Reformed Epistemology
and the Problem of Religious Diversity

Reformed Epistemology
and the Problem of Religious Diversity

Proper Function, Epistemic Disagreement,
and Christian Exclusivism

JOSEPH KIM

☞PICKWICK *Publications* · Eugene, Oregon

REFORMED EPISTEMOLOGY AND THE PROBLEM
OF RELIGIOUS DIVERSITY
Proper Function, Epistemic Disagreement, and Christian Exclusivism

Pickwick Publications
An Imprint of Wipf and Stock Publishers
199 W. 8th Ave., Suite 3
Eugene, OR 97401

www.wipfandstock.com

ISBN 13: 978-1-60899-511-0

Cataloging-in-Publication data:

Kim, Joseph.

    Reformed epistemology and the problem of religious diversity : proper function, epistemic disagreement, and christian exclusivism / Joseph Kim.

    xiv + 110 p. ; 23 cm. Including bibliographical references.

    ISBN 13: 978-1-60899-511-0

    1. Reformed epistemology. 2. Religious pluralism—Christianity. I. Title.

BL51 .K50 2011

Manufactured in the U.S.A.

This book is dedicated to my wife Juliet.

Contents

Preface / ix

Acknowledgments / xi

Abbreviations / xiii

1   Introduction / 1

    Identifying the Problem / 2
    The Moral and Epistemic Objection / 6
    Prospectus / 16

2   Warrant, Proper Function, and Christian Belief / 18

    Proper Function and Design Plan / 18
    An Objection to Externalism: Bonjour / 24
    An Objection to Externalism: Bonjour on Armstrong / 27
    A Proper Function Response to Bonjour's Counterexample / 32
    Perception and Proper Function / 33
    The Extended A/C Model and Proper Function / 40

3   Epistemic Disagreement and the Equal Weight Theory / 46

    Epistemic Disagreement: Kelly / 49
    Two Additional Cases / 58
    The Equal Weight Theory / 60
    The Problem of Religious Diversity and the Equal Weight Theory / 63

4   The Great Pumpkin Objection / 66

    The Nature of Defeaters / 66
    The Son of Great Pumpkin Objection: Martin and DeRose / 70
    The Son of Great Pumpkin Objection: A Response / 77

5   The Internalist Criterion and the Inadequacy Thesis / 82

    Reformed Epistemology and the Internalist Criterion: Willard / 82
    Reformed Epistemology and the Internalist Criterion: A Response / 89
    The Inadequacy Thesis: Baker / 94
    The Inadequacy Thesis: A Response / 96

6   The Central Issue of Religious Exclusivism / 100

Hick on the Central Issue of Religious Exclusivism / 100
Retrospection / 106

Bibliography / 109

Preface

THIS BOOK IS AN investigation into an issue at the intersection of epistemology, the philosophy of religion, and religious pluralism: the problem of religious diversity. The problem of religious diversity claims that in cases of peer disagreement with respect to religious beliefs, one should give equal weight to the opinion of an epistemic peer (someone who is alike epistemically in every way in terms of intelligence, honesty, thoroughness, exposure to the issues, etc.) and to one's own opinion. Given this, mutually exclusive religious propositions serve as defeaters for one another. A belief P defeats belief Q if P gives one a good reason to give up belief Q, thus it is not tenable to hold to any one particular religious proposition over another. If the argument for the problem of religious diversity is sound, then this is a serious problem for the Christian exclusivist.

The primary thesis of my book is that the problem of religious diversity does not succeed in providing a defeater for Christian exclusivism. In arguing against the problem of religious diversity, I offer a Reformed Epistemological defense of Christian belief. Rather than reference a single argument, Reformed Epistemology is the stance that belief in God is properly basic. This is the view that one need not give a positive argument for the existence of God to be warranted in holding the belief that God exists. Reformed Epistemologists typically reject evidentialism, the view that one cannot hold to any religious belief unless there is conclusive evidence for it. The most prominent defenders of Reformed Epistemology include philosophers such as Alvin Plantinga, William Alston, and Nicholas Wolterstorff. This book's focus will be on the epistemological issues concerning Plantinga's account of warrant as proper function in connection to his defense of Christian belief.

Warrant is that quality and quantity that distinguishes knowledge from mere true belief. A true belief must be warranted to count as an instance of knowledge since true beliefs that are only accidentally true do not count as knowledge. Plantinga construes warrant in terms of proper functionality. A belief B has warrant for subject S if and only if the relevant processes that produce belief B are functioning properly in a cognitive environment sufficiently similar to that for which S's faculties are designed; and the modules of the design plan governing the production of B are (1) aimed at truth, and (2) such that there is a high objective probability that a belief formed in accordance with those modules (in that sort of cognitive environment) is true. Plantinga argues that a properly functioning cognitive faculty can produce warranted Christian beliefs.

There have been a number of objections to Plantinga's defense of Christian belief, the majority of which are aimed at his account of warrant as proper function. Some of the more well known objections seem to argue that Plantinga's defense fails because of his epistemic externalism, and thus seem to presuppose that epistemic internalism is required to provide a tenable defense of Christian exclusivism. Other objections argue that Plantinga's defense is incoherent and claim that mutually exclusive religious belief systems can utilize Plantinga's defense of Christian belief to argue for their own religious belief system. Throughout this book, I will argue that none of these objections succeed in providing a defeater for Plantinga's Reformed Epistemological defense of Christian belief.

I have tried to organize this book so that anyone with an interest in the topic, including professors and students, may benefit from the discussion. Since chapters 2, 4, and 5 are more technical, someone without much background in philosophy can start with chapters 1, 3, and 6 before turning to the more technical chapters. Where relevant, I have tried to explain some of the more technical words in the footnotes section for those who are unfamiliar with the philosophical terms used by epistemologists.

Acknowledgments

The ideas in a book are rarely or perhaps never developed in isolation. I'd like to thank Thomas Blackson, Stewart Cohen, and Steven Reynolds who provided much valuable feedback on an earlier version of this work. In particular, Steven Reynolds's incisive and penetrating comments have contributed greatly to this book. If there is any philosophical merit to this book, it is primarily due to his excellent questions and comments. I also owe a great intellectual debt to Alvin Plantinga for the subject matter of this book. Although he was never my teacher in the ordinary sense, I have learned more from him on the subject of philosophy (in particular epistemology) than anyone else.

I would also like to thank the following organizations for their support during the writing of this book: Baylight, Binnerri EM, Cornerstone, CPC, Evergreen, First Harvest, Grace, Gracepoint, Hope, KAPCA, Karis, Milal, NCA, New Life, Open Door, Precision Ferrites, Redeemer, Sarang SD, and True North. I'd also like to thank the students, staff, and faculty members of キリスト聖書神学校 (Christ Bible Seminary) for their encouragement during the writing of this book. In addition, I'd like to offer my sincere thanks to the many individuals (too numerous to name) who have also supported me during the writing of this book. My parents James and Susan, and my brother David have given me encouragement beyond belief. I wish to thank them for their generous love.

Finally, my wife and children deserve the bulk of my gratitude. My two sweet sons were a constant source of joy and delight by their smiles and laughter. They were a constant reminder to me that there are things much more important than writing a book. My wife Juliet deserves the majority of my gratitude. Through her encouragement, support, exhortation, and love I hope to one day become something more than a resounding gong or a clanging cymbal. I dedicate this book to her.

Joseph Kim
Nagoya, Japan

Abbreviations

The symbol '~' will be used to indicate 'it is not the case that.' So ~X means it is not the case that X.

CE   Christian Exclusivism = CE_1 + CE_2

CE_1: The world was created by God, an almighty, all-knowing and perfectly good personal being (the sort of being who holds beliefs, has aims and intentions, and can act to accomplish these aims).

CE_2: Human beings require salvation, and God has provided a unique way of salvation through the incarnation, life, sacrificial death, and resurrection of his divine son.

PRD   The argument for the problem of religious diversity

AP   Abstemious Pluralism. If S knows that others don't believe p (and, let's add, knows that he can't find arguments that will persuade them of p), then S should not believe p.

AP´   If S knows that others don't believe AP (and, let's add, knows that he can't find arguments that will persuade them of AP), then S should not believe AP.

PC   If Christian belief (CE) is true, then Christian belief is likely to be warranted.

SD   *sensus divinitatis*

Z   The mere existence of epistemic peers who disagree is not sufficient as a reason for one to give up one's belief or retreat into skepticism/agnosticism.

GPO   The Great Pumpkin Objection

SGP   The Son of the Great Pumpkin Objection

PQ   Keith DeRose's Anti-Plantinga argument

WP   Julian Willard's primary argument

IT   Inadequacy Thesis

NAT   Negative Apologetic Thesis

1

Introduction

THE WORLD DISPLAYS A very large variety of religious and anti-
religious ways of thinking, with most of them pursued by people
of great intellect and seriousness. Consider the many varieties of beliefs
that go under the names Hinduism or Buddhism, and the difficulty
of categorizing such sects. Or even among theistic religions, there are
many different types of beliefs that go by the names Christianity, Islam,
or Judaism. There are also large varieties of beliefs that are essentially
non-spiritual in nature such as Confucianism, that still fall under the
category of religious belief. Consider what is said on the topic of religious diversity by the Stanford Encyclopedia of Philosophy:

> Religious diversity exists most noticeably at the level of basic the-
> istic systems. For instance, while within Christianity, Judaism, and
> Islam it is believed that God is a personal deity, within Hinayana
> (Theravada) Buddhism God's existence is denied and within
> Hinduism the concept of a personal deity is, in an important
> sense, illusory. Within many forms of Christianity and Islam, the
> ultimate goal is subjective immortality in God's presence, while
> within Hinayana Buddhism the ultimate goal is the extinction
> of the self as a discrete, conscious entity. However, significant,
> widespread diversity also exists within basic theistic systems. For
> example, within Christianity, believers differ significantly on the
> nature of God. Some see God as all controlling, others as self-
> limiting, and still others as incapable in principle of unilaterally
> controlling any aspect of reality. Some believe God to have in-
> fallible knowledge only of all that has occurred or is occurring,
> others claim God also has knowledge of all that will actually oc-
> cur, while those who believe God possesses middle knowledge

add that God knows all that would actually occur in any possible context.[1]

Add to this pantheon of religious diversity the areligious: those who reject religious belief. Amidst this backdrop in contemporary philosophy of religion there has been much debate about whether one can defend any form of religious exclusivism, the view that the religious propositions (or some of the religious propositions) of one religion are true. The debate typically asks whether mutually exclusive religious beliefs provide a defeater for the religious propositions of any one particular religion.[2] I will argue no. In this chapter, I will describe some of the general issues surrounding religious exclusivism before turning more specifically to Alvin Plantinga's Reformed Epistemological defense of Christian belief from this charge.

IDENTIFYING THE PROBLEM

One can construe religious exclusivism in many different ways, but my concern is with the Christian exclusivist. Consider the two most basic Christian propositions that most Christians believe are true (together known as CE):[3]

CE₁ The world was created by God, an almighty, all-knowing and perfectly good personal being (the sort of being who holds beliefs, has aims and intentions, and can act to accomplish these aims).

CE₂ Human beings require salvation, and God has provided a unique way of salvation through the incarnation, life, sacrificial death, and resurrection of his divine son.

Some Christian exclusivists defend CE by offering arguments for the truth of CE₁ and/or CE₂. Consider the following summary of such an argument given by Thomas Aquinas:

---

1. Stanford Encyclopedia of Philosophy, "Religious Diversity."

2. A defeater as I use it here is simply a belief P that is incompatible with another belief Q, such that given P, one cannot rationally hold to Q. Thus belief in Q is defeated by belief P.

3. Plantinga, *Warranted Christian Belief,* 438. He refers to CE₁ and CE₂ as 1) and 2) in his book.

1. Nothing can move itself.

2. If every object in motion had a mover, then the first object requires a mover.

3. No movement can go on for infinity.

4. Therefore, there must be a first unmoved mover.

5. The first unmoved mover is God.

Regardless of whether one is convinced by this argument or not, Aquinas is arguing for the conclusion that God exists. To be sure there are evidentialist arguments that are considerably more sophisticated, but the general idea is the same. Namely, that a sound argument can be given that concludes that God exists.

The Reformed Epistemologists, unlike Aquinas, reject the notion that one can offer a sound argument for the conclusion that God exists. They believe (as we shall see) that belief in God is properly basic and one can hold to belief in God as true without offering an argument for the truth of God's existence. Plantinga in his Reformed Epistemological defense of Christian belief makes it clear that he will not be able to argue for the truth of CE in such a way that those who do not already hold to CE as true will accept the premises of his argument.[4] Yet, he believes that CE is true.

As we shall see, Plantinga argues that *if* Christian belief (or CE) is true, then Christian belief is likely to be warranted. In arguing for this conditional conclusion, we see that he also argues for the claim that the variety of mutually exclusive religious beliefs to Christian belief does not provide a defeater for CE. Plantinga further clarifies his Christian exclusivist views by adding a few conditions to the acceptance of CE. Someone does not count as a Christian exclusivist unless:[5]

(i) they are fully aware of other religions,

(ii) they are aware that there is genuine devotion and piety in the other religions,

(iii) and they know of no argument that would convince all or most of these other intelligent adherents of other religions and the anti-religious to their own exclusivist position.

4. As Plantinga does, I will use "Christian belief" synonymously with "CE."

5. Plantinga, *Warranted Christian Belief*, 440.

What sets this sort of Christian exclusivism apart from many other Christian exclusivists who hold to CE is condition (iii). This type of Christian exclusivist holds his ground that CE is true, even if he cannot produce an argument that shows that all mutually exclusive propositions to CE are false.

A major objection to any form of religious exclusivism is the problem of religious diversity. The objection can be formulated into an argument (PRD):

1. There are a large variety of mutually exclusive religious propositions held by a large variety of religious believers and non-believers.[6]

2. The believers and non-believers in premise 1 are epistemic peers, people who are alike epistemically in every way given the particular belief in matters of intelligence, honesty, thoroughness, exposure to question/research/data, etc.

3. One should give equal weight to all of the religious propositions in premise 1 because they come from epistemic peers.

4. Given 3, these mutually exclusive religious propositions serve as defeaters for one another.

5. Therefore, it is not tenable to hold to any one particular religious proposition in any exclusive sense.

6. Therefore, any form of religious exclusivism is unwarranted.

I will reply to this argument by arguing against premises 3 and 4.

Religious exclusivism, like many issues in the philosophy of religion, is a controversial issue so it is important to make clear what I will be defending and what I will not be defending. My main argument will take the following form:

1. If Plantinga's proper function account is a reasonable account of warrant, then rival religious views to CE do not serve as a defeater to Christian belief having warrant.

---

6. I count areligious propositions as religious propositions. So propositions such as "God does not exist," or "there is no good we know of that would justify God in allowing evil if God were absolutely good" count as religious propositions since they are concerned with religious belief or unbelief.

2. If rival religious views to CE do not serve as a defeater to Christian belief having warrant, then Plantinga's Reformed Epistemological defense of CE is reasonable.

3. Therefore, if Plantinga's proper function account is a reasonable account of warrant, then Plantinga's Reformed Epistemological defense of CE is reasonable.

Plantinga assumes that religious propositions are no different from scientific or philosophical propositions in that they have a truth-value: true or false. I will refer to all religious claims and propositions in the same manner that Plantinga does. I will not defend the concept of God in Christian belief nor will I defend the use of Christian scripture. Rather, my goal is to defend CE from PRD.

There are two additional issues surrounding PRD that I will not be defending. First, I will not be arguing for the truth of CE. My goal will be to defend Christian exclusivism against the more narrow charge that rival religious views count as an epistemic defeater for the rationality of Christian belief as construed in CE given Plantinga's proper function account of warrant. My defense, thus, will be an *epistemic* defense and not a metaphysical one. A metaphysical defense would require something much more than what I hope to defend, namely something beyond claiming that X does not serve as a defeater for Y given Z.

Second, I will not be defending or presenting any views that hold to a non-realist conception of truth. Although the nature of religious truth can be very complex given the varied ways of viewing God and ultimate reality, I will assume that religious propositions have a truth-value in much the same way that non-religious propositions have a truth-value. Hence, I will be ignoring or putting by the wayside any objection that rejects the principle of non-contradiction. Furthermore, I will not be considering any emotivist views on religious truth and language. Emotivist views typically claim that religious propositions (or judgments) are simply expressions of one's own attitude.[7] Though there are interesting questions to be pursued in this sort of non-realist context, I will not be dealing with them in this work. Finally, I will not be considering any non-cognitivist views on religious propositions and language. On this view, which is distinct from the view that religious truth is an expression of emotions, religious propositions fail to express anything at all—either

---

7. For an example of emotivism, see Ayer, *Language, Truth, and Logic.*

true or false—they are more like music.[8] I will be putting by the wayside any such view that is non-cognitivist in nature.

Finally, certain religious traditions claim that religious claims are non-propositional or argue for a non-realist pluralism. This is to claim that a religious statement does not always have a truth-value or a religious statement can have differing truth-values. For example, one Hindu may claim that "God exists" is true. Another Hindu, may claim that "God exists" is false. A third Hindu may claim that both of the previous aforementioned views are correct, since the principle of non-contradiction does not apply at all times to religious statements. Although there are interesting questions to be pursued here with respect to religious claims, I will not be pursuing them. My focus will be on whether someone can hold to CE as true given that there are mutually exclusive religious claims by epistemic peers that contradict or are inconsistent with CE. PRD, as an epistemic objection, presupposes that religious propositions can have truth-values in the same way any other propositions about the external world can have truth-values. Thus my focus will solely be on whether mutually exclusive religious beliefs serve as a defeater for CE given Plantinga's proper function account of warrant. This endeavor then takes for granted or presupposes that religious propositions are no different than non-religious propositions with respect to truth.

THE MORAL AND EPISTEMIC OBJECTION

We are now in a position to turn to the primary focus of my project. Does the fact that there are religious propositions that contradict CE provide a defeater for CE? Plantinga argues no. He goes further and claims that even if one is unable to give an argument for the truth of CE that would convince those who reject CE, one can still be reasonable in holding to CE as true. Of course Plantinga also claims that those who reject CE are also unable to offer an argument for the falsity of CE in such a way that those who accept CE would accept the premises of such an argument.[9]

8. For an example of a non-cognitivist ontology see Carnap, "Empiricism, Semantics, and Ontology." According to Carnap, we can generate a framework for language such that certain propositions can be deemed necessary given the particular rules of the language. So what is "true" or "false" is simply a byproduct of the particular necessary propositions given the language constructed, rather than any correspondence to some fact about the universe construed via a realist picture of the universe.

9. I use the term non-exclusivist to denote any religious position that rejects religious exclusivism; including inclusivist, pluralist, pantheist, or even atheist. Of course

Plantinga's initial defense of Christian exclusivism is to defend religious exclusivism from two primary objections: the Moral Objection and the Epistemic Objection. I will consider each of these in turn.

The Moral Objection claims that there is a "self-serving arbitrariness, an arrogance or egoism" when anyone accepts propositions such as CE.[10] Plantinga concedes that anyone who holds to CE as true is going to claim that someone who believes something incompatible with CE is mistaken and believes something that is false. She also believes that those who do not believe as she does with respect to CE, fails to believe something that is true. Consider an example of someone who levels this sort of moral objection against the religious exclusivist:

> ... except at the cost of insensitivity or delinquency, it is morally not possible actually to go out into the world and say to devout, intelligent, fellow human beings ... we believe that we know God and we are right; you believe that you know God, and you are totally wrong.[11]

There are a few key assumptions working here in this sort of moral objection even if one tones down the rhetoric. We see this sort of charge would not work for just any case where someone believes something and others disagree. For example, it wouldn't work in politics. Imagine that one endorses a particular political view, X. If someone simply disagreed with you, and gave you reasons why they disagreed, one would be obstinate to consider that person arrogant, insensitive, or delinquent. What is the difference then between politics and religious claims? Perhaps one clue is that the moral objector against the religious exclusivist is presupposing that if there is a God, then everyone has equal or similar access to God[12]. Hence the claim that one cannot claim to know God while rejecting the claim that others know God equally well. The key in this particular objection seems to be the claim that no one person has some sort of exclusive *privileged access* to religious truth in rejecting the religious beliefs of others as false. Plantinga concedes that of course the

---

someone can be a religious exclusivist (Islam, etc.) without being a Christian exclusivist and someone can hold to Christian Belief, including CE, without holding to Plantinga's Reformed Epistemological views.

10. Plantinga, *Warranted Christian Belief*, 443.

11. Cantwell Smith, *Religious Diversity*, 14.

12. Not all religious exclusivists are theists in the strict sense, so although I use the term "God" one could make the same case for the term "religious truth."

exclusivist *does see* herself as privileged in terms of her religious beliefs, but this does not mean that she should be subject to this objection.

Plantinga argues in the following way:

(1) If this moral objection charge is correct, there must be some possible way to correctly adjust one's beliefs so as to rid oneself of the defect (i.e., ought implies can, etc.)

(2) There are only two responses to (1). Either a) believe the negations of the exclusivist beliefs, or b) abstain from believing both the exclusivist beliefs and the negations of the exclusivist beliefs, assuming we have set aside non-cognitive and anti-realist views on religious truth and religious propositions.

(3) If one chooses a) and believes the negations of the exclusivist beliefs, this still leads to exclusivism.

(4) If one chooses b) and abstains from believing both the exclusivist beliefs and the negations of the exclusivist beliefs, they are still claiming their "abstaining from belief" is privileged in the same manner as the exclusivist or those in a).

(5) There is no way to avoid the moral objection against exclusivism regardless of what position one takes, including non-exclusivism or abstaining from belief. Hence the moral objection is mistaken.

So regardless of one's doxastic state with respect to any set of religious propositions, whether an exclusivist or non-exclusivist, Plantinga claims that one cannot avoid the moral objection (on a realist account of religious propositions). Hence, the moral objection is faulty at its core.

Consider premise (3). If one believes the negations of the exclusivist beliefs, then one is still holding to propositions that others don't believe. This of course doesn't put this person in a better position than the religious exclusivist with respect to the charge of arrogance or egoism as the moral objection claims. The religious non-exclusivist here holds to certain propositions not held by others, hence she is in the same position as the exclusivist. This is no objection at all against the exclusivist, since the non-exclusivist who holds to the denials of the propositions held by the exclusivist would fall prey to the same objection or charge.[13] The key for

---

13. Certain non-exclusivists deny that religious propositions are held to the same standards as philosophical propositions and advocate a non-realist position. Whether this can be shown to the satisfaction of those who disagree is another matter, since this

this sort of objection to religious exclusivism, as we have seen earlier for the one leveling this sort of charge at the exclusivist, is *privileged access* to religious truth. The religious exclusivist, at least the religious exclusivism that Plantinga defends, claims a sort of privileged access to God (and hence, religious truth) that the non-exclusivist lacks. The non-exclusivist in leveling this sort of charge rejects that the religious exclusivist has privileged access to religious truth. The moral objection seems to hold muster only if one assumes that the exclusivist and non-exclusivist have equal access to religious truth. Premise (3) simply claims that the non-exclusivist, if she believes in the negations of the exclusivist beliefs, is also holding to an exclusivism of sorts. Of course if that is the case, then it's not exclusivism the moral charge is leveled at but something entirely different and the objection loses its force. What of the one who suspends judgment on the issue? They would have to suspend judgment on both the views of the exclusivist and the non-exclusivist. As we shall see in the next section, I will argue that the one who suspends judgment is still endorsing a form of exclusivism—that is she holds certain religious propositions to be true and better supported than other ones.

Consider premise (4), the abstemious pluralist. This person withholds or abstains belief in both the exclusivist propositions and their negations. Plantinga characterizes the abstemious pluralist position (AP) as such:

> If S knows that others don't believe p (and, let's add, knows that he can't find arguments that will persuade them of p), then S should not believe p.[14]

Suppose the abstemious pluralist holds to AP. Of course he will recognize that not everyone holds to AP, and will have no argument—at least no argument that would convince most of those who disagree—that will change the minds of those who disagree with AP. He too is holding to a particular exclusive proposition, namely AP, which others reject.

Plantinga stops here, but suppose we go further. Suppose we substitute p in AP for AP itself. Then we have the following: (AP′)

would put the person under the same moral objection of arrogance as the exclusivist since she still holds a position (i.e., that of a non-realist view of truth with regard to religious propositions, etc.) that others reject.

14. Plantinga, *Warranted Christian Belief*, 446.

> If S knows that others don't believe AP (and, let's add, knows that
> he can't find arguments that will persuade them of AP), then S
> should not believe AP.

Of course if AP were true, then AP′ would also be true. If AP′ were true, then one should not believe AP. Hence, AP falls on itself and rejects itself as a principle. The Moral Objection claims that there is a "self-serving arbitrariness, an arrogance or egoism" when a religious exclusivist rejects propositions such as P, since the religious exclusivist neglects the important point that there are others who don't accept propositions such as P. The abstemious pluralist abstains from believing both the exclusivist propositions and their negations. Plantinga is claiming that the abstemious pluralist position is also an exclusivism of sorts, that is the abstemious pluralist holds to some religious propositions as true and holds other ones as false. If that is the case, then he is in the same boat epistemically as the others in claiming his position is privileged. So the abstemious pluralist, in the end, has either the option of 1) continuing to endorse AP, which leads to AP′ which in turn leads to a rejection of AP, or 2) claim that her position is privileged, which is to give up her abstemious pluralism. Either way, her position is not a tenable one.

Perhaps the abstemious pluralist can object that Plantinga has miscategorized their claims and made their objection unnecessarily weak, a straw man objection. The abstemious pluralist may reject the claim that simply abstaining from believing both the exclusivist beliefs and their negations is truly a privileged position as premise (4) claims. Perhaps they may want to claim that theirs is an agnostic position of sorts, one where they believe there is not enough evidence or argument to accept the views of either the religious exclusivist or the non-exclusivist. The position is more a state of suspended belief rather than endorsing the views of the religious exclusivist or the non-exclusivist. Consider an example. Suppose you are an abstemious pluralist and are unsure whether a particular proposition X or its negation ~X is true.[15] After examining the evidence, you are still unsure where the evidence leads. Thus you suspend judgment with respect to X or ~X. The abstemious pluralist would have to hold to one of these three propositions regarding X:

---

15. The symbol ~ is the negation symbol, so ~X is equal to it is not the case that X or simply not-X.

1. X is true.

2. X is false.

3. I am unsure whether X is true or false and will abstain from believing in X or ~X.

The abstemious pluralist obviously holds to 3. How does she arrive at 3, rejecting 1 and 2? It's not for lack of knowledge on the topic. Rather it's the evidence (or the lack thereof) that leads her to 3, instead of 1 or 2.[16] Is position 3 any different from 1 and 2? The religious exclusivist holds to 1 because she believes the evidence leads her to position 1. Some religious non-exclusivists hold to position 2 because she believes the evidence leads her to position 2. The abstemious pluralist seems to hold to her position in the same manner. She is using her cognitive faculties in the same manner as the religious exclusivist and the non-exclusivist. She holds to the position that seems best to her given her assessment of the evidence or lack thereof.

The sort of abstemious pluralist that is being targeted is, as Plantinga stipulated earlier, someone who is aware of the religious diversity in the world and admits that people in the other religions display as much devotion and piety as she does. If someone who is familiar with the arguments for positions 1 and 2 still chooses 3, she must have a reason to choose 3. Even if her reason is that positions 1 and 2 are equally weak or strong, that is still evidence that leads her to position 3. The Moral Objection claims that there is a "self-serving arbitrariness, an arrogance or egoism" when anyone accepts propositions such as P. The abstemious pluralist is claiming that any religious view that claims they are privileged over another view is to be rejected. So whether in the strong sense as Plantinga has pointed out earlier or in the weaker sense as I have pointed out here, the abstemious pluralist seems unable to escape the claim that even abstaining from belief is still a claim that one's position is privileged. If this is the case, then the abstemious is still no different from our exclusivist.[17] The abstemious pluralist holds to a particular proposi-

16. I use the word evidence in the broadest sense here. For example, someone may not have evidence in the sense of a philosophical argument that there exist minds other than her own but this does not show there is no evidence at all. Perhaps direct awareness or sense perception may also fall in this category, evidence that is not the result of an argument.

17. Some philosophers take an even stronger route and claim there is no such thing as religious pluralism. Although it is not my intention to defend such a claim, some have

tion that she sees as privileged over others based on the evidence, which is precisely why she can launch an objection over positions 1 and 2. The abstemious pluralist holds to a position that is really no different than the ones held by the religious exclusivist and the non-exclusivist.

The second objection to religious exclusivism that Plantinga describes is the epistemic objection. The epistemic objection to religious exclusivism argues that Christian exclusivism is unjustified. The epistemic objection takes this general form:

1) The Christian exclusivist who holds to conditions (i)–(iii) violates certain epistemic duties.

2) The religious exclusivist is intellectually arbitrary.

3) Therefore, the religious exclusivist is unjustified in her condition.

Consider premise 1), that the Christian exclusivist violates epistemic duties and is not within her intellectual rights in holding to her religious exclusivism. This charge presupposes that the views of the exclusivist and the non-exclusivist are on epistemic par. For if they were on par with one another, the exclusivist would be either stubborn or irrational in holding to her beliefs and claiming the denials of her beliefs are false. The religious exclusivist would seemingly need a good argument then to distinguish her position from that of the non-exclusivist or else her position is arbitrary.

A good argument has to be valid of course, and also must not be circular or beg any questions against those with whom one disagrees. What of the premises? If the argument is valid, then the premises must also not be circular or beg any questions against those with whom one disagrees. A good argument must also be cogent, since the goal of such an argument would be to distinguish one's own position from that of one's opponents. (I will set aside the claim that a good argument need not be persuasive since the opposition may hold false beliefs.) The goal of a good argument for religious exclusivism would be to show the non-exclusivist that the views of the religious exclusivist are epistemically privileged. On such an account, if the argument consists of premises that are not accepted by those who disagree, then I won't have a right

---

argued that there are only exclusivist religious views since every religious view is going to claim some religious propositions as true that are denied in other religious belief systems. See D'Costa, "Impossibility of a Pluralist View of Religions."

to accept these premises either based on this charge of epistemic parity unless I have another argument for those premises. Then we'd have to come up with another argument for the argument that one gave for the original premises, since the premises of the new argument would not be accepted by those who disagree. And so on, ad infinitum. If this is what one means by violating one's epistemic duty, the argument is lacking. Plantinga says of this that:

> The result seems to be that my duty precludes my being party to any *ultimate* disagreements, at least any *ultimate* disagreements of which I am aware, and at least as far as decisive assent goes. Can that be right? Perhaps there is no way you can find moral common ground with a member of the Ku Klux Klan. Perhaps you can't find any premises you both accept that will serve in a good argument for your views against his. Would it really follow that you don't have a right to give decisive assent to the proposition that racial bigotry is wrong? Hardly.[18]

So even if epistemic duties do exist as described, the religious exclusivist does not hold to a position that is significantly different from the religious non-exclusivist. Like the non-exclusivist, the religious exclusivist would think long and hard about her position and appeal to her epistemic community in much the same way the non-exclusivist would. She, like the non-exclusivist, would think her conclusions were correct even if there were others who dissent. She could not be shirking a duty since she is doing exactly what the non-exclusivist does in forming his position, or if she is shirking a duty, the non-exclusivist would also be shirking the same duty. Hence, the charge that the exclusivist violates some epistemic duty is mistaken, since the non-exclusivist seems to be in the same position.

Consider premise 2), that the exclusivist position is intellectually arbitrary. The charge is that when the exclusivist prefers her own religious propositions based on her own religious views, there will be epistemic parity among her beliefs and those who disagree with her. However, both the exclusivist and the non-exclusivist would have nearly the same internal markers, including devotion, intelligence, inner experience, etc. The Christian exclusivist we are concerned with already concedes (iii) that any non-exclusivist (and also the exclusivist for a rival religion who rejects CE) would display the same internal markers with

18. Plantinga, *Warranted Christian Belief*, 450.

respect to devotion, piety, and the like. Of course even in conceding this point, the Christian exclusivist need not claim that her beliefs are on par epistemically with those who reject CE. Consider an example that Plantinga gives.

Suppose you and a colleague are in dispute over whether it is morally right to advance one's career by lying. Suppose further that the colleague is an epistemic peer, someone who displays as much intelligence as you do and has thought about the issue with as much concern as you have, etc. You of course think that your beliefs are epistemically privileged, that is you believe that your colleague's position is immoral even though both of you display nearly identical internal markers with respect to the issues of morality. Does the mere fact that she holds that she is right give you a good reason to abandon your belief that it is morally wrong to advance one's career by lying? Of course not. You would think your colleague had some moral blind spot, or she was raised in a particular environment that led to such a blind spot, etc. You would think that you were privileged in your position even when you couldn't show to the satisfaction of your colleague that you are right and she is wrong via an argument. Plantinga claims in such a case that "the believer in question doesn't really think the beliefs in question are on a relevant epistemic par" even though the opposing party may share very similar internal markers.[19] So the fact that the non-exclusivist has the same internal markers as the exclusivist does not show that their positions are epistemically identical or that the religious exclusivist is being arbitrary in holding to her belief. This is true even if, as we have seen, the religious exclusivist cannot produce an argument that would satisfy those who disagree with her that she is in fact epistemically privileged.

The abstemious pluralist believes that it is better to withhold judgment. Of course others disagree, and those that disagree would have the same internal markers of justification as the abstemious pluralist. The assumption here is that the internal markers are the same for everyone. Premise 1) of the epistemic objection claims that the Christian exclusivist violates certain epistemic duties. This seems to presuppose that the internal markers are the same, hence the exclusivist has the same epistemic duties as the non-exclusivist. If the internal markers are the same, then the abstemious pluralist seems to be no better off than the exclusivist. Even though the Christian exclusivist could be wrong in

19. Ibid., 453.

holding P as true, this could also be so for the non-exclusivist in holding to his belief. As we have seen earlier, this is also true of the abstemious pluralist.[20] Hence, a fallibilism with respect to religious propositions need not lead one to skepticism on all religious propositions. From a neutral vantage point one could be wrong in holding to an exclusivist position with respect to epistemic duty, intellectual arbitrariness, and internal markers. Of course this is also true of the non-exclusivist and the abstemious pluralist position as well. If the internal markers are not the same, then one could not really claim that the exclusivist violates certain epistemic duties. How could one launch this sort of objection when the internal markers are totally different in the absence of any argument? After all, the exclusivist does claim that her views are privileged in that she believes what is true and those that do not believe what she believes, believes something that is false. The non-exclusivist also does the same. Hence, it's not problematic to claim that one can reasonably hold to one's religious exclusivism even when one *cannot* produce an argument (or knows of no argument) that would convince all or most of those who disagree.

Finally, Plantinga notes that a religious exclusivist's confidence may be reduced once she encounters the religious diversity that exists in the world but it need not do so via arguments. Consider what he says of this:

> Since degree of warrant depends in part on degree of belief, it is possible, though not necessary, that knowledge of the facts of religious pluralism should reduce his degree of belief and hence the degree of warrant that P can have for him; it can deprive him of knowledge of P. . . . Things *could* go this way with the exclusivist. On the other hand, they *needn't* go this way.[21]

It may even be that the knowledge of the facts of religious pluralism can increase the warrant that a Plantinga-exclusivist has in CE, since the mere knowledge of this could serve as an occasion for a renewed and

---

20. I'm presupposing here that both the non-exclusivist and the abstemious pluralist hold to certain religious propositions. I define religious propositions as those that affirm or reject religious belief. The non-exclusivist holds to the negations of the religious exclusivist's propositions. The abstemious pluralist also holds to certain religious propositions on this view, including "there is equally good evidence for or against P" or "there is no good evidence for P or against P," etc.

21. Plantinga, *Warranted Christian Belief*, 457. Plantinga's emphasis.

more powerful working of the belief-producing processes by which she has come to believe CE in the first place. As we shall see, Plantinga labels this belief-producing faculty the *sensus divinitatis* (sense of divinity). For if there were a *sensus divinitatis*, then the knowledge of the facts of pluralism could trigger a more powerful working of the process by which one comes to have religious (or Christian) beliefs.

It need not go this way but according to Plantinga it could, if Christian belief were true and warranted in the way that he has (as we shall see) outlined. Plantinga concludes that mere knowledge of religious diversity need not reduce a Christian exclusivist's confidence in her religious exclusivism. His strategy is to argue that if the Christian exclusivist's cognitive faculties are functioning properly, then her Christian beliefs would likely be warranted if true.

PROSPECTUS

In this first chapter, my goal was to try and isolate some of the key issues surrounding CE and PRD. My intention for this chapter was merely to lay out some preliminary issues before a more detailed defense of my thesis. My goal for this work is to offer a more detailed defense of Plantinga's Reformed Epistemological defense of CE from the problem of religious diversity.

My strategy will be as follows. In chapter 2, I will argue that Plantinga's argument for Christian belief is tied to his account of warrant as proper function. I try to motivate the first premise of my main argument, by claiming that warrant as proper function is a reasonable account of warrant. In chapters 3, 4, and 5, I defend the second premise of my main argument: if rival religious views to CE do not serve as a defeater to Christian belief having warrant, then Plantinga's Reformed Epistemological defense of CE is reasonable. In chapter 3, I specifically argue against the third premise of PRD, the equal weight view. Proponents of the equal weight view claim that in cases of peer disagreement, one should give equal weight to the opinion of an epistemic peer and to one's own opinion. I argue that the equal weight view is mistaken. I will also argue that the claim that CE is not defensible due to its multiple competitors is mistaken because of its dependence on the equal weight view. In chapters 4 and 5, I take up the notion of defeaters and argue against some prominent objections to Plantinga's Reformed Epistemology and warrant as proper function. I argue that these objections do not serve as defeaters to Christian exclusivism. Finally in chapter 6, I consider the central issue of exclusivism and conclude that it is reasonable to claim that if a proper function account is a reasonable account of warrant, then Plantinga's Reformed Epistemological defense of CE is reasonable. This of course does not entail that CE is true nor that Christian belief is in fact warranted.

2

Warrant, Proper Function, and Christian Belief

Is it possible for someone to hold to Christian belief while displaying proper cognitive function? Plantinga argues yes. In this chapter I will explore Plantinga's arguments in answering this question. First, I will present Plantinga's warrant-as-proper function account. Next, I will turn to Bonjour's anti-foundationalist argument which argues against externalist species of epistemic justification before turning to a response the proper functionalist might give as an externalist. My goal is to explicitly connect Plantinga's warrant as proper function account with his defense of Christian exclusivism. Finally, I will then apply the warrant-as-proper-function account to both perceptual belief and Christian belief.

PROPER FUNCTION AND DESIGN PLAN

Warrant for Plantinga is that quality and quantity that distinguishes knowledge from mere true belief. It is not merely a quality but a quantity since warrant also comes in degrees. Why use the term warrant rather than the more universal term justification? Justification suggests a sort of epistemic duty or requirement and is deontological in nature. One can trace this to Descartes and Locke, both of whom explain justification in terms of fulfilling one's epistemic duties or satisfying one's epistemic obligations.[1] For some philosophers, justification simply *is* warrant and a deontological conception of justification is used synonymously with warrant. One of the keys for this is the connection between deontological conceptions of justification and internalist accounts of warrant. For our purposes, the internalist is someone who claims that warrant conferring properties are internal to the knower. Some prominent internalist

---

1. Plantinga, *Warranted Christian Belief*, 4.

accounts of justification simply construe warrant as justification in terms of epistemic duty or requirement. The knower then, on these accounts, always has cognitive access to the warrant and properties that ground it. Fulfilling one's epistemic duties regarding a particular belief is only possible if one has access to the warrant and properties that ground that belief, thus the direct connection between deontology and most internalist accounts of justification.

The externalist denies the internalist thesis that one always has access to the warrant and the properties that ground it for a particular belief and claims that warrant supervenes on properties that the knower may or may not have any epistemic access to.

As we shall see, Plantinga's warrant as proper function account and his defense of Christian belief is clearly externalist in nature. The warrant as proper function account is externalist since it denies that one *always* has access to the warrant and the properties that ground it.[2] Consider Plantinga's four conditions that are required for warrant:

1) One's cognitive faculties must function properly,

2) one's cognitive environment has to be sufficiently similar to the one for which the cognitive faculties were designed,

3) the design plan that governs the production of such beliefs is aimed at producing true belief, and

4) the design plan is a good one such that there is a high statistical (or objective) probability that a belief produced under these conditions will be true.

What does it mean for 1) a cognitive faculty to function properly? Consider a few examples here. Imagine going to the doctor and he tells you that your thyroid gland is not functioning properly, its output of thyroxin is low. So he prescribes you some medication that will remedy your situation. A thyroid gland is functioning properly if it outputs a certain amount of thyroxin. It is not functioning properly if its output of thyroxin is too low or too high. Likewise, a cognitive faculty has a proper function in the way it outputs beliefs given its environment. Consider

2. An externalist may argue that in *some* situations one can have cognitive access to the warrant and the properties that ground it, while the internalist will argue that one *always* has cognitive access to the warrant and the properties that ground it. Externalism, again, is simply a denial of internalism and hence is the weaker thesis of the two.

someone who sees white and black as red. So he will point to all instances of white, black, and red colors and call them 'red.' His visual faculties are functioning properly with respect to that which is red, and are not functioning properly with respect to that which is white or black. This is because someone with properly functioning visual faculties will be able to point out and differentiate instances of red from those that are white or black. This person is unable to do so since his visual faculties are not functioning properly. Proper functionality works much the same way for epistemic faculties as it does for other things.[3] A properly functioning cognitive faculty or person will respond in a particular way in particular situations in coming to certain beliefs. As we shall see however, condition 1) is necessary but not sufficient for a cognitive faculty to function properly.

Consider condition 2), one's cognitive environment has to be sufficiently similar to the one for which the cognitive faculties were designed. What does it mean for a cognitive faculty to be designed or to have a design plan? Plantinga claims that "a thing's design plan is the way the thing in question is 'supposed' to work, the way in which it works when it is functioning as it ought to, when there is nothing wrong with it, when it is not damaged or broken or nonfunctional."[4] Humans and natural organisms have design plans, as do computers and automobiles. Our cognitive faculties have a design plan in the same way any scientific organism has a design plan. For example, if the design of one's lungs is the oxygenation of blood throughout the body, the design plan is for the lungs to inhale oxygen and exhale carbon dioxide. A design plan then is such that it facilitates optimal design in terms of the evolutionary process.[5] Based on our design plan, we find our faculties responding to the circumstances around us in our particular environment: if our cognitive faculties are functioning properly, then under certain conditions we form certain beliefs. So another way of viewing one's design plan is to view it in terms of optimal function given the way the cognitive faculty is supposed to work.

3. Plantinga, *Warranted Christian Belief*, 5–6.

4. Ibid., 21.

5. Ibid., 13. Optimal design in this sense is different from claiming that our cognitive faculties points to a designer. Our design plan could be naturalistic, theistic, or even non-theistic. Plantinga's point is simply to claim that our design plans facilitate what is optimal in terms of the evolutionary process.

Given this, the particular environment for which one's cognitive faculties were designed (or an environment sufficiently similar to the one for which they were designed) plays a crucial role in the proper functioning of a cognitive faculty. Suppose that you have a cognitive check-up with some of the world's leading cognitive scientists, and they all declare that you are in superb epistemic condition. Suppose further, without your knowledge, that at the instant after your check-up you were somehow transported to a planet that revolves around the star Alpha Centauri. Unbeknownst to you, it feels the same in every respect as earth so that you are unaware that you are on this planet rather than on earth. On this planet there are elephants that are invisible and make no noise when they walk, but they emit a sort of radiation that is lacking on earth so that you hear what sounds like a trumpet every time one of these elephants is nearby. Suppose that one of these elephants is nearby and you hear something that sounds like a trumpet even though you don't see anything around you. You form the belief that there must be a trumpet nearby. There is nothing wrong with your cognitive faculties. In fact, as the cognitive scientists declared, they are functioning properly. However, your belief that a trumpet is sounding nearby has no warrant.

You may be justified in your belief in this case, and you have violated no epistemic duties, and you are well within your epistemic rights to hold this belief and you are completely rational in holding this belief, yet the belief has no warrant for you.[6] The belief has no warrant even though you may be justified in having fulfilled your epistemic duties. Although your cognitive faculties are in perfect working order, they are not attuned to the particular environment you find yourself in. So the proper functioning of one's cognitive faculties is necessary, but not sufficient for warrant since one also needs to be in an environment that is sufficiently similar to the one for which our cognitive faculties were designed. In the case of the Alpha Centauri elephants, the problem was not with one's cognitive faculties but rather the environment. They are in the wrong environment given their particular design plan. One needs the right sort of environment for that cognitive faculty based on the given design plan.[7]

Condition 3), connected to 2), is the notion that that the design plan of the cognitive faculty that governs the production of beliefs needs

6. Ibid., 6–7.
7. Ibid., 7–11.

to be such that it is successfully aimed at producing true beliefs. This is because proper function and the right sort of environment for a cognitive faculty, though necessary, are still not sufficient for warrant. The fact that a cognitive faculty is to be successfully aimed at truth is something distinct from merely providing us a survival advantage. Consider a rabbit whose faculties give off a warning that there is a predator nearby whenever the rabbit hears any sudden noise. It may be that 99.9 percent of these noises are false alarms, but the fact that the rabbit acts on all of them and runs away ensures its survival. Still, this is not a faculty that is aimed at true beliefs. Unless the cognitive faculties are successfully aimed at true beliefs rather than mere survival as in the case of the scared rabbit, they would not be functioning properly. Hence, the beliefs produced by a faculty that is not successfully aimed at true beliefs would not be warranted just as the rabbit is not warranted in thinking that just *any* noise is a predator—though this ensures its survival.

We now turn to condition 4), the design plan of our cognitive faculties must be a good one so that there is a high objective or statistical probability that a belief produced by a properly functioning faculty will be true. The cognitive faculties, of course, must be reliable.[8] Imagine a well meaning but incompetent angel, one of Hume's infant deities, who designs a variety of rational persons such that the design is a real failure, the persons hold beliefs but most of them are false. Conditions 1)–3) are satisfied, yet there is no warrant on this picture since the reliability condition or 4) must also be met. That is, even though conditions 1)–3) are satisfied and one has a true belief, one wouldn't have Plantinga-warrant until condition 4) is also satisfied. The key question is: how high does the reliability need to be in terms of objective probability? This is a vague notion according to Plantinga. One's cognitive faculties need not be infallible to be considered reliable or functioning properly.

Consider the example of Frege who produced a set of axioms for set theory such that for any property P there exists a set of those things that have P. Bertrand Russell pointed out to Frege that this axiom along with others yields a contradiction. If this axiom is true, then there will be a set of non-self membered sets that will both be a member of itself and not be a member of itself. This, Plantinga points out, is "wholly unacceptable behavior for a set."[9] Even though Frege was a logician of great magnitude

8. Ibid., 17–20.
9. Ibid., 19.

and his cognitive faculties were functioning properly and highly reliable, they were still not immune from error even though there was a very high objective probability that Frege's conclusions on set theory were correct. Perfect reliability, then, is not necessary on this view. Plantinga-warrant then requires a design plan such that there is a high objective probability that the belief be true. However, it does not follow from this that one's cognitive faculties be immune from error for the cognitive faculty to function properly. If not perfect reliability, how high precisely? Plantinga claims that what we have here is vagueness:

> I say the presupposition of reliability is a feature of our usual way of thinking about warrant; but of course this presupposition is not inevitable for us. The skeptic, for example, can often best be seen as questioning this presupposition.[10]

The answer is that there is no answer with regard to how high the reliability must be, at least no answer that would satisfy the skeptic's demands. We presuppose our cognitive faculties are reliable, and we find ourselves warranted even if the skeptic denies this.

So we see that an approximate working definition of Plantinga's proper function as warrant account is as follows:

> A belief *B* has warrant for subject *S* if and only if the relevant segments (the segments involved in the production of *B*) are functioning properly in a cognitive environment sufficiently similar to that for which *S*'s faculties are designed; and the modules of the design plan governing the production of *B* are (1) aimed at truth, and (2) such there is a high objective probability that a belief formed in accordance with those modules (in that sort of cognitive environment) is true.[11]

A belief has Plantinga-warrant if and only if it is produced by cognitive faculties functioning properly (subject to no cognitive malfunction) in a cognitive environment congenial for those faculties, according to a design plan successfully aimed at truth. The focus here is on the particular cognitive faculty functioning properly rather than the fulfilling of any epistemic duties.

---

10. Ibid., 19–20.
11. Ibid., 19.

With this brief account of Plantinga-warrant and the pillars that support it (proper function and the design plan), I turn to a few potential internalist responses.

AN OBJECTION TO EXTERNALISM: BONJOUR

Laurence Bonjour has given several well-known and influential arguments against the adequacies of any externalist theory of justification. He categorizes internalism as such:

> The most generally accepted account ... is that a theory of justification is *internalist* if and only if it requires that all of the factors needed for a belief to be epistemically justified for a given person be *cognitively accessible* to that person, internal to his cognitive perspective.[12]

As we shall see, Bonjour equates a theory of justification as "at least approximately correct" in terms of what distinguishes knowledge from mere true belief.[13] So justification as Bonjour uses it is at least approximately close to what Plantinga labels warrant. Bonjour offers the following argument against any externalist theory of justification that he labels the anti-foundationalist argument:

(1) Suppose that there are *basic empirical beliefs*, that is empirical beliefs (a) which are epistemically justified, and (b) whose justification does not depend on that of any further empirical beliefs.

(2) For a belief to be epistemically justified requires that there be a reason why it is likely to be true.

(3) For a belief to be epistemically justified for a particular person requires that this person be himself in cognitive possession of such a reason.

(4) The only way to be in cognitive possession of such a reason is to believe *with justification* the premises from which it follows that the belief is likely to be true.

(5) The premises of such a justifying argument for an empirical belief cannot be entirely *a priori*; at least one such premise must be empirical.

---

12. Bonjour, "Externalism/Internalism," 132.
13. Bonjour, *Structure of Empirical Knowledge*, 3.

(6) Therefore, the justification of a supposed basic empirical belief must depend on the justification of at least one other empirical belief, contradicting (1); it follows that there can be no basic empirical beliefs.[14]

We see that premise (3) is the internalist premise, since the justification (or warrant as Plantinga uses it) must be cognitively accessible to the person.[15] Bonjour concedes this seems to be question begging against the externalist, since premise (3) takes internalism as a premise for an argument against externalism. Bonjour also concedes that this argument won't really convince any externalist to reject externalism, since he uses internalism in one of its premises, namely premise (3). His strategy, as we shall see, is to offer something on an intuitive level.

The externalist will reject premise (3), since for the externalist it is not necessary that the person for whom the belief is basic, "know, or justifiably believe the premises of such an argument."[16] According to Bonjour, the externalist foundationalist faces two connected problems: 1) he would have to avoid any requirement that would further justify one's alleged basic empirical beliefs as true, since that would negate their status as basic, while 2) still maintaining the connection between justification and truth. Bonjour categorizes the externalist response to these connected problems as such:

> … there must indeed exist a reason why a basic empirical belief is likely to be true (or even, in some versions, guaranteed to be true), the person for whom the belief is basic need not himself have any cognitive grasp at all of this reason (thus rejecting premise (3) of Bonjour's anti-foundationalist argument).[17]

The key for the externalist, according to Bonjour, is that the justification for a basic belief must have an appropriate relationship to the truth. The relationship then between the basic belief and truth is such that it must either be highly probable that the basic belief is true or it must be nomologically certain. Granted, if known, the justification for the basic belief would provide an excellent reason for one to accept the basic belief but one need not have any cognitive grasp of this reason

14. Ibid., 32.

15. Note that premise 2 in Bonjour's argument here requires a connection to truth, which is more specific than the general definition of internalism.

16. Bonjour, *Structure of Empirical Knowledge*, 33.

17. Ibid., 34.

in order to be justified in their basic belief. The justification of a basic belief need not involve any other beliefs, hence there is no justification-transfer between another belief and the basic belief. This is the solution to the foundationalist problem typically given by externalists, hence externalists reject (3).

Bonjour's primary concern is with externalist foundationalist views that aim to solve the epistemic regress problem. Consider a belief P. Usually one shows that P is justified inferentially via another belief Q, so P should be accepted on the basis of Q. Of course Q would have to be justified for one to accept P. Where does Q get its justification? One can trace this inferentially to another justified belief R. And so on ad infinitum. This is the epistemic regress problem. A solution to this problem: basic beliefs that are justified without involving any inferential justification from other beliefs. Though Bonjour's attacks are not directed towards Plantinga's proper function account, they are still a critique of Plantinga's view that can be labeled a moderate foundationalist external-ist view.[18] This is because a properly functioning cognitive faculty can produce warranted (or justified as Bonjour seems to use the term) be-liefs without consciously accessing the warrant for the belief. Bonjour's attacks on externalism apply to all forms of externalism that claim that one can have basic beliefs that are justified or warranted without involv-ing any inferential justification/warrant from other beliefs – including Plantinga's warrant-as-proper-function account.

---

18. Ibid., 26. Bonjour further states that, "According to moderate foundationalism, the noninferential warrant possessed by basic beliefs is sufficient by itself to satisfy the adequate-justification condition for knowledge. Thus on this view, a basic belief, if true, is automatically an instance of knowledge (assuming that Gettier problems do not arise) and hence fully acceptable as a premise for the justification of further empirical beliefs. By virtue of their complete justificatory independence from other empirical be-liefs, such basic beliefs are eminently suitable for a foundational role. Moderate founda-tionalism, as the label suggests, represents a relatively mild version of foundationalism. Historical foundationalist positions typically make stronger and more ambitious claims on behalf of their chosen class of basic beliefs." Bonjour further points out that noth-ing about foundationalism itself rests on the infallibility of basic beliefs, hence strong foundationalism is philosophical overkill. That is, one need only defend moderate foun-dationalism for foundationalism itself to be tenable, hence his attacks are focused on moderate foundationalism.

AN OBJECTION TO EXTERNALISM: BONJOUR ON ARMSTRONG

One prominent externalist view that Bonjour argues against is one held by David Armstrong.[19] Armstrong, like any externalist foundationalist, views the justification of a basic belief as being dependent on a particular external relation between the belief and the world. This connection Armstrong refers to as a "thermometer model" of non-inferential knowledge. Just as a reliable thermometer reflects the temperature, so does one's basic beliefs reflect the states of affairs which makes them true. How so? Via a law-like connection, where "a state of affairs Bap (such as a's believing that p) and the states of affairs which makes 'p' true, such that, given Bap, it must be the case that p."[20] Bonjour categorizes Armstrong's views as such, "what ultimately justifies a belief is some appropriate set of facts which are (in the most typical case) external to the believer's conception of the situation."[21]

Now, Armstrong's concern is clearly knowledge while Bonjour is concerned with justification. However, Armstrong wants to claim that the beliefs which satisfy his criterion are epistemically justified or rational. So someone whose beliefs satisfy these conditions would have a reliable cognitive faculty in the same way a thermometer is a reliable instrument. This is the sort of reliability that Armstrong has in mind when he claims that a cognitive faculty must be reliable. Of course not all thermometers are in fact reliable, and even reliable thermometers are not accurate 100 percent of the time or are only accurate under certain conditions. So Armstrong also claims that:

> . . . a noninferential belief is justified if and only if there is some property H of the believer, such that it is a law of nature that whenever a person satisfies H and has that belief, then the belief is true.[22]

This connection between the belief and the particular state of affairs which makes the belief true is limited to "that of a completely reliable sign to thing specified."[23] This is so that Armstrong can exclude cases

---

19. Armstrong, *Belief, Truth, and Knowledge.*
20. Ibid., 166.
21. Bonjour, *Structure of Empirical Knowledge,* 33.
22. Armstrong, *Belief, Truth, and Knowledge,* 197.
23. Ibid., 182.

where the belief itself may be the cause of the particular state of affairs which makes it true, since that would not yield knowledge.

Bonjour sees little hope for the sort of externalism advocated by Armstrong. He notes that as an advocate of internalism it is problematic to argue against any form of externalism, including Armstrong's version, since the externalist would surely reject an appeal to premises that Bonjour would offer as an internalist. So Bonjour will proceed on an intuitive level, and though these intuitions may not be conclusive in terms of being an objection to externalism, he hopes to show that the burden of proof is on the externalist to show that she is in fact correct.

Consider this case, given by Bonjour, in which he claims all of Armstrong's criteria are met:

> Norman, under certain conditions which usually obtain, is a completely reliable clairvoyant with respect to certain kinds of subject matter. He possesses no evidence or reasons of any kind for or against the general possibility of such a cognitive power or for or against the thesis that he possesses it. One day Norman comes to believe that the President is in New York City, though he has no evidence either for or against this belief. In fact the belief is true and results from his clairvoyant power under circumstances in which it is completely reliable.[24]

Does Norman's belief that the President of the United States of America is in New York City have enough justification for knowledge in this case? Bonjour argues no.

Suppose that Norman believes, in fact, that he does have clairvoyant powers and that this contributes to his belief that the President is in New York City. Bonjour claims it is obviously irrational for someone to believe they have such powers when, given the stipulations of the case, they have no evidence or reasons for or against the thesis that he possesses it. If his belief that he has clairvoyant powers is unjustified, then so must his belief about the President being in New York City since the latter belief depends on the former according to the stipulations of the case.

Suppose that Norman however does not believe that he has clairvoyant powers. This would mean that Norman has no good reason at all for thinking that the President is in New York City. Why would he maintain the belief that the President is in New York City? He would

---

24. Bonjour, *Structure of Empirical Knowledge*, 41.

not maintain such a belief since there is no way for him to know the President is in New York City without the use of clairvoyance, which he has no evidence for or against. Bonjour conjectures that this simple fact of Norman not having evidence for or against clairvoyance is probably enough for him to cease having a belief about the President's whereabouts. That is, there is no reason for Norman to hold such a belief since there is no evidence for or against clairvoyance and there is no other way to know about the President's whereabouts according to the stipulations of the case. If Norman does hold the belief, then we would deem him epistemically irresponsible if one assumes a deontological view of epistemic justification. Hence, Norman would not be justified in holding to the belief. This is because according to Bonjour, it is "part of one's epistemic duty to reflect critically upon one's beliefs, and such critical reflection precludes believing things to which one has, to one's knowledge, no reliable means of epistemic access."[25] The critical claim here by Bonjour is that the mere fact that an external relation holds and the belief happens to be true does not equate to an epistemically justified belief when the particular relation is entirely outside one's ken.

On Armstrong's externalism, Norman would be like a thermometer cognitively speaking. Consider Armstrong's thermometer model where via a law-like connection, "a state of affairs Bap (such as a's believing that p) and the states of affairs which makes 'p' true, such that, given Bap, it must be the case that p."[26] If we substitute the case above we have the following:

> Via a law-like connection, Norman's believing that the "President is in New York City" and the states of affairs which make the "President is in New York City" true is such that given Norman's believing that the "President is in New York City," it must be the case that the "President is in New York City."

So if Norman does have property H, the property of being a completely reliable clairvoyant under the particular existing conditions and arriving at the belief on that basis, then he holds the belief in question only if it is true.[27] Bonjour claims of this that "Norman does have property H and

25. Ibid., 42.

26. Armstrong, *Belief, Truth, and Knowledge*, 166.

27. Bonjour, *Structure of Empirical Knowledge*, 43.

does hold the belief in question; therefore, the belief is true."[28] Suppose an external observer constructed this particular justifying argument. The external observer would be able to justify *his own* acceptance of such a belief with the same content, since Norman (according to Armstrong's thermometer model) could be used as an epistemic instrument of sorts for such an observer. However, Bonjour points out that clearly this does not justify Norman's own acceptance of his belief that the President is in New York City.[29] Bonjour argues that Norman cannot have the viewpoint of an external observer, and the simple fact that it is potentially available to him does not justify his own acceptance of the belief.

Bonjour argues it is necessary that the believer in this situation must know or "at least justifiably believe" some set of such premises or reasons to be in position himself to offer the justification for the belief.[30] Bonjour claims this general requirement would be waived by the externalist:

> The externalist position seems to amount to merely waiving this general requirement in a certain class of cases, and the question is why this should be acceptable in these cases when it is not acceptable generally. If it were acceptable generally, then it seems likely that any true belief would be justified, unless some sever requirement were imposed as to how available such premises must be; and any such requirement seems utterly arbitrary, once the natural one of actual access by the believer is abandoned.[31]

Thus, Bonjour concludes that externalism is not only an *ad hoc* solution to the epistemic regress problem but is false.

It is not an accident that Norman's belief about the President's whereabouts is true since the original case stipulates that Norman is clairvoyant, though he possesses no evidence for or against clairvoyance and his having the ability of clairvoyance. This however, does not justify Norman's own belief according to Bonjour. From Norman's own subjective perspective it seems right but he is unable to say why, so the belief seems unjustified. So Bonjour concludes that the rationality or justifiability of a person's belief (in this case Norman's) should be judged from the person's perspective rather than one which is not available to him, that of the external observer. The external observer is able to see that

28. Ibid.
29. Ibid.
30. Ibid.
31. Ibid.

Norman has property H—that of being a completely reliable clairvoyant under the existing conditions and arriving at the belief on that basis, whereas Norman is unable to see such a property since the relation in question is entirely outside his ken. Bonjour sees this as an intuitively compelling argument. However, he does see that it is still fairly close to what an externalist would simply deny right off the bat so he considers some other intuitions. I will turn now to what I believe to be the stronger of the two examples that Bonjour gives against externalism.[32]

Consider the connection between knowledge and the rational actions of an agent. Imagine if our clairvoyant Norman believes (in addition to his belief about the President's whereabouts) that the Attorney General is in Chicago. Unlike the belief about the President, the belief about the Attorney General's whereabouts is due to ordinary empirical evidence and not clairvoyance. If Norman had to bet his life on the whereabouts of either the President or the Attorney General, it is obvious that Norman would choose the whereabouts of the Attorney General. If that's the case, on externalism we end up with this strange account where it is "more rational to act on a merely reasonable belief than to act on one which is adequately justified to qualify as knowledge (and which in fact *is* knowledge)."[33] Bonjour contends that the belief about the Attorney General's whereabouts is more reasonable epistemically for Norman than the belief about the President's whereabouts, yet according to externalism the latter belief is the one that constitutes knowledge since clairvoyance is quite highly reliable (according to the case) even if Norman isn't aware of any evidence for or against the existence of or the reliability of clairvoyance. So the externalist in this case would have to accede that Norman should act (even in the case where his life depends on it) on the belief about the President rather than the belief about the Attorney General. This is untenable according to Bonjour, but would be a position that falls out of externalism. Even though Bonjour concedes that he would not have convinced the externalist to change her intuitions on the matter, he claims that his examples show that the burden of proof is now on the externalist to show how his position could better accommodate such an example.

---

32. Ibid., 44–45. The first analogy concerns a moral analogy to epistemic externalism, my focus will be on the second.

33. Ibid., 45 (Bonjour's emphasis).

A PROPER FUNCTION RESPONSE
TO BONJOUR'S COUNTEREXAMPLE

Bonjour asked this question previously about externalism: why should the mere fact that an external relation obtains confer justification for a subject when the relation in question is "entirely outside his ken"? As Bonjour notes, this question doesn't amount to much more than a denial of the externalist's primary claim. Hence, his concerns are with burden of proof issues based on intuitions about the Norman case. One externalist strategy may be to respond: why isn't Norman's belief justified on an externalist account? This strategy would be to push Bonjour on his intuition that Norman's belief is not justified.

Let N = Norman's belief that the President is in New York City and P = the belief (which he may or may not have) that Norman has clairvoyant powers. Bonjour argues that Norman's belief is not justified by the following dilemma: a) either Norman has belief P or b) Norman does not have belief P. Consider a) Norman has belief P. Belief P would lack justification on most versions of externalism, even if Norman does have clairvoyant powers, since the case stipulates there is no evidence for or against any type of clairvoyancy. That is, there is no reason for anyone to hold that such a belief exists, including Norman himself. Belief P would not be justified. This lack of justification for belief P would apply to all beliefs generated by Norman's clairvoyant faculty, including the belief that N. So N wouldn't be justified either on this account. Externalists of course would want to know how N was formed. For example, was belief N generated by a reliable process? If so then the belief could be justified, if not then no. Of course if the belief is justified, then this goes against Bonjour's claim that Norman's belief is not justified. If the belief is not justified, then externalist accounts seem to generate the correct result: namely that belief N is not justified.

Consider b) that Norman does not have belief P. If he doesn't have beliefs about P, why would he believe any thoughts at all about the President based on something he's not even aware of? He simply would not have a belief that the President is in New York City. Although Bonjour stipulates that Norman does have such a belief, if belief P is not justified as I have argued above, Norman would not have such a belief that the President is in New York City. So though Bonjour wants to claim that Norman's belief N is in fact justified on the assumption that he has the belief N, if belief P is not justified then he wouldn't have any such beliefs about N at all. So it would seem that on either a) or b) that N is not justified.

Even if Armstrong's version of externalism is mistaken, Plantinga's proper function account seems to accommodate the Norman case quite well, at least as well as Bonjour's. We see that a belief has Plantinga-warrant if and only if it is produced by cognitive faculties functioning properly (subject to no cognitive malfunction) in a cognitive environment congenial for those faculties, according to a design plan successfully aimed at truth. On a proper function account of warrant, there is a distinction between clairvoyance cases such as Norman's and more ordinary cases of sense perception. Norman would not be warranted (or justified as Bonjour seems to use the term) in his belief since it might be the case that clairvoyant faculties are not governed by any design plan. Perhaps no evolutionary process has made Norman to have such a faculty. Of course more normal perceptual faculties can and do, when functioning properly, generate warranted (or justified) beliefs.

Bonjour does seem correct then, that anyone offering an argument based on an appeal to intuitions given by a case such as Norman's would not offer much in terms of a conclusive argument against those who do not already presuppose that internalism is true. The Norman example is given to highlight an intuition, as Bonjour concedes. He also correctly points out that any committed externalist would reject his appeal to any premises that he could offer as an internalist, including his anti-foundationalist argument stated earlier. Of course it's also true that any committed internalist would also surely reject an appeal to premises that an externalist would offer. Bonjour's Norman case, while interesting, does not shift the burden of proof to the externalist since Plantinga's proper function externalism is able to account for such a case like Norman. I will now turn to Plantinga's account of perception given his warrant as proper function account.

PERCEPTION AND PROPER FUNCTION

A perceptual belief for Plantinga counts as knowledge if and only if that perceptual belief is true, sufficiently strong (as a perception), and is produced by cognitive faculties that are successfully aimed at truth and functioning properly in an epistemic environment that is right for a creature with the sort of perceptual powers that Norman has.[34] Plantinga thinks

---

34. Plantinga, *Warrant and Proper Function*, 89.

that many of our perceptual beliefs do meet this criteria and hence have enough warrant to constitute knowledge. Consider Bonjour's Norman and his clairvoyance case. Would Norman's clairvoyance satisfy these conditions? Put another way, is Norman's clairvoyance belief true, sufficiently strong (as a perception), and produced by cognitive faculties that are successfully aimed at truth and functioning properly in an epistemic environment that is right for a creature with the sort of perceptual powers that Norman has? The answer is no. It is not in Norman's design plan, on Plantinga's account, to be clairvoyant because his design plan is the same as ours. Or perhaps the clairvoyancy would be integrated with his other abilities and needs according to his design plan and so he would be aware of his abilities. In either case, Norman's clairvoyance would not satisfy these conditions for perceptual warrant.

Some have argued however, that these perceptual conditions are rarely met. This sort of perceptual skepticism, of course, cannot really be answered by giving any sort of argument since there would be no premises that one could offer the perceptual skeptic that the latter would accept as firmly as perceptual skepticism itself. Plantinga's account is not to answer the skeptic by giving an argument whose premises the skeptic accepts, but rather argue that warrant for our perceptual beliefs come in the basic way. Consider something like modus ponens.[35] We take modus ponens to be warranted, even if we can't show that it is in fact a valid form of argument apart from appealing to itself. Again, if someone denies that modus ponens is valid what would one appeal to in showing that it indeed is valid? None could be given apart from modus ponens itself, which our skeptic already rejects. Likewise, what could one offer the perceptual skeptic? Not much. Plantinga claims that perceptual beliefs have warrant in the basic way even if one has no argument for their perceptual beliefs.[36]

Does perceptual warrant come in degrees? Plantinga answers yes. Suppose I see something that looks like a car coming towards me in a

---

35. Modus ponens is typically an argument of this form: 1) If A, then B. 2) A. 3) Therefore, B.

36. For a similar account, see Burge, "Perceptual Entitlement." Burge defends an externalist account of perceptual warrant which he labels "entitlement." Burge argues that certain higher-level animals and young children are entitled to hold to their perceptual beliefs even though the warrant for their beliefs does not lie in the space of reasons and arguments. He argues against a view where the only sort of epistemic warrant for perception must lie within the space of reasons. His account is externalist in nature.

dense fog and I form the belief that I see a car. This belief is only minimally warranted. However, the car starts approaching me so I am only a few feet away from the car and I form the belief that I see a car. This second belief is now highly warranted, enough so that I can claim that I have knowledge of the proposition "there is a car before me." The difference in degrees of warrant between the first and second car beliefs is not strengthened (or weakened) by any argument or appeal to shared premises. The two key features for Plantinga with respect to perceptual warrant is 1) perceptual experience, and 2) the proper basicality of perceptual beliefs. I now turn to both of these key features in order.

First, we see that experience plays a role in perceptual knowledge. Consider our car example again. Imagine seeing a car in dense fog. One has a *sensuous* experience of the car in that one is appeared to in a certain way: whitish, brownly, grayly, blackly, etc. It is difficult to describe such an experience in purely sensory terms. Perhaps it may take a lot of skill and training to be able to accurately describe one's sensuous experiences. Plantinga notes there is another type of experience involved in such a circumstance: nonsensuous experience.[37] This is the experience of forming such a belief under the appropriate conditions. Consider an example. I see a car in the fog and something about the experience feels right. It is not an impulsion or push towards feeling that way, since the belief comes about much too quickly. I see that it is a car and I know something tells me it's the right belief even though there is a dense fog. This is a nonsensuous experience since there seems to be something else besides the mere sensuous experience of whitish fog and the color of the car, etc.[38] Perhaps a nonsensuous experience is not an experience in the same sense as a sensuous experience, but rather a phenomenal accompaniment in terms of forming the belief or having the particular belief.[39]

The key for Plantinga is that there is something beyond the mere sensuous experience, regardless of how one describes it. So in such a situation we have: 1) the sensuous experience, 2) the nonsensuous experience, and 3) the belief formed. If one forms a belief that there is a tiger rather than a car in the car situation, then one would display cognitive dysfunction. There is nothing illogical about the presence of a tiger in such a situation—perhaps there is a zoo nearby and a tiger has

37. Plantinga, *Warrant and Proper Function*, 92.
38. Ibid.
39. Ibid.

escaped and is in the dense fog. However, having experienced cars and tigers in different settings, proper functionality requires a more narrow set of doxastic responses given the particular sensuous experience. If my cognitive faculties are functioning properly, in one set of circumstances I form the belief there is a tiger and in another set of circumstances I form the belief there is a car. One would have to be malfunctioning cognitively to interchange these beliefs in the given circumstances when one clearly sees a car.[40] In forming perceptual beliefs, there seem to be multiple ways (even if the doxastic responses are narrow) that a properly functioning cognitive faculty can generate beliefs.

The second key feature of perceptual beliefs for Plantinga is that they are properly basic. A properly basic belief is a belief whose warrant does not come via argument or inference from other propositions. A properly basic perceptual belief is not warranted via any beliefs based on the experience, rather its warrant comes from the belief itself. Self-evident beliefs fall under this category, for example $1 + 1 = 2$. These beliefs are accepted not on the basis of argument or inference to other beliefs, but are basic in nature and accepted without appeal to argument or inference to other beliefs. A properly basic belief can have very high degrees of warrant according to Plantinga. Perceptual beliefs fall under this category; they can have very high degrees of warrant even though they are properly basic. Plantinga says of the proper basicality of a perceptual belief that:

> My being appeared to in that way under those circumstances (including the circumstance of proper function, and the other conditions necessary for warrant) is what confers warrant. My *having* that sort of experience in those circumstances helps confer warrant upon the belief in question; it does not acquire its warrant by being believed on the basis of propositions *reporting* that experience.[41]

The circumstance itself does not give warrant to the belief, but the warrant is conferred in the basic way when one finds oneself in the particular circumstance of holding the belief. Thus there is no warrant transfer from one belief to another. The appropriate circumstances include whatever conditions are necessary for warrant. In a properly basic belief, there is

40. Ibid., 93.
41. Ibid., 95.

no evidence that one can point to as a reason to be warranted in holding that belief.

Consider our car example again. One sees a red car approaching after the fog has cleared. In this situation, one doesn't ordinarily infer that one sees a red car from being appeared to in a particular way. One also does not form the belief that "there is a red car" on the basis of some other evidence. So one does not typically first note that "I see a reddish blockish thing" and then reason from that belief to the belief that one sees a red car. Rather one forms a belief by simply *seeing* the car as it is. It is not an inference from "I see a reddish blockish thing" to "it's a red car." Rather, one forms the latter belief by simply seeing the car. No inference is involved from being appeared to in a particular way. Typically, a perceptual belief is formed in this way.

Forming a belief about one's experience, however, seems much more indirect. One could first see an object several hundred feet away, and then after seeing the object form the belief that "I see the object." Although one could form beliefs about one's experiences in this way, perhaps something like "I am appeared to in that way," this is typically not the case with perceptual beliefs. One does not ordinarily form beliefs describing one's experience when one has a perceptual belief, the perceptual beliefs are held in the basic way.[42] However, if one is asked *why* do you see that particular object? One may cite experience as a reason, but it does not follow from this that one accepts that belief on some sort of evidential basis.

The key here on this view is that the warrant for the perceptual belief comes from the belief being formed in the appropriate sort of circumstances. Plantinga claims that one can say that it is *occasioned* rather than caused by the circumstances, which can include one having the right sort of experience (i.e., being appeared to in a particular way). However, it is not required for one to actually *believe* that one has the experience in question for the perceptual belief to have warrant, it is basic in nature.[43] Furthermore, (echoing Thomas Reid) Plantinga claims that even if one does believe that they are being appeared to in a particular way it isn't necessary that one has to believe on any sort of evidential basis for the belief to have warrant.[44] Why doesn't the experience itself count as evi-

42. Ibid.

43. Ibid, 96.

44. Thomas Reid (1710–1796) was a Scottish philosopher who endorsed a common sense philosophy.

dence? Consider a typical perceptual belief (ex. the red car example earlier), there is no warrant transfer in that I go from a) a proposition that I
generate from the experience, to b) my belief. I simply find myself having
the belief in question. I do not reason or infer from any evidence and
then hold the belief based on the experience itself or seeing a blockish
reddish thing. The beliefs are not evidentially supported by propositions
about my immediate experience; I hold them in the basic way.[45]

Perceptual beliefs then can have high degrees of warrant; regardless of the evidential support the particular proposition has regarding
one's immediate experience. This does not mean that basic beliefs are
incorrigible. The main requirement for perceptual warrant would be
that a particular perceptual faculty's design plan be successfully aimed
at truth. A belief gets warrant in the basic way under the appropriate
circumstances if this type of belief production is in our design plan. So
if our perceptual faculties are functioning properly in accordance with
our design plan, we will form a particular sort of response in a particular
situation given a particular epistemic environment governed by a design
plan that is successfully aimed at truth. This is when our perceptual beliefs have warrant in the basic way.

If we recap Plantinga's four conditions for proper functionality, as
applied to our perceptual faculties, we have:

1) One's perceptual faculties must function properly,

2) one's perceptual environment has to be sufficiently similar to the
   one for which the cognitive faculties were designed,

3) the design plan that governs the production of such beliefs is
   aimed at producing true belief, and

4) the design plan is a good one such that there is a high statistical (or objective) probability that a belief produced under these
   conditions will be true.

What does it mean for 1) a perceptual faculty to function properly? A
perceptual faculty has a proper function in the way it outputs beliefs
given its environment. Consider again the person who sees white and
black as red. So he will point to all instances of white, black, and red
colors and call them "red." His visual perceptual faculties are functioning properly with respect to that which is red, and are not functioning

---

45. Plantinga, *Warrant and Proper Function*, 96.

properly with respect to that which is white or black. This is because someone with properly functioning visual perceptual faculties will be able to point out and differentiate instances of red from those that are white or black. This person is unable to do so and is not functioning properly. A properly functioning perceptual faculty will respond in a particular way in particular situations in coming to certain beliefs. As we shall see however, 1) is necessary but not sufficient for a perceptual faculty to function properly.

Condition 2) states that: one's perceptual environment has to be sufficiently similar to the one for which our perceptual faculties were designed. As was noted earlier, a design plan is the way the thing in question is supposed to work such that it facilitates optimal design in terms of the evolutionary process.[46] Based on our design plan, we find our perceptual faculties responding to the circumstances around us in our particular environment. If our perceptual faculties are functioning properly, then under certain conditions we form certain beliefs. Suppose you see an ophthalmologist who says you are in superb condition with respect to your visual perceptual faculties. Suppose further that you are transported to a dark cave filled with bats. While the bats are able to navigate through the cave with their perceptual faculties, you are unable to. It is totally dark to you and you are unable to see. There is nothing wrong with your visual faculties, they are functioning properly but are simply not in an environment for which they were designed. One needs the right sort of environment for that perceptual faculty based on the given design plan to have warranted beliefs.[47]

Condition 3), connected to 2), is the notion that that the design plan of the perceptual faculty that governs the production of beliefs needs to be such that it is successfully aimed at producing true beliefs. The fact that a perceptual faculty is successfully aimed at truth is something distinct from merely providing us a survival advantage. Consider a fish whose visual perceptual faculties give off a warning whenever they see the color red, which is the color of their primary predator. It may be that 99.9 percent of all the red they see are false alarms, but the fact that the fish acts on all of them and swims away ensures its survival. Still, this is

46. Ibid., 13. As explained earlier, optimal design in this sense could be naturalistic in nature, theistic, or even non-theistic. Plantinga's point is simply to claim that it indeed facilitates what is optimal in terms of the evolutionary process.

47. Ibid., 7–11.

not a faculty that is aimed at true beliefs. Hence, the beliefs produced by such a faculty would not be warranted just as the fish is not warranted in thinking that just *any* instance of the color red is a predator though this ensures its survival.

We now turn to condition 4), the design plan of our perceptual faculties must be a good one so that there is a high objective or statistical probability that a belief produced by a properly functioning faculty will be true. Suppose someone is unknowingly drugged so that they see the entire world in black and white every few seconds, and then back to normal in full color, and then in black and white, and so on. Suppose further that every time you go from seeing the world in black and white to normal, you are unaware of the switch. Suppose you see a dark purple object in front of you when you see in color, and then you see the object as black, and then back to dark purple, and so on. Conditions 1)–3) of Plantinga-warrant are satisfied, yet it's clear there is no warrant on this picture since the reliability condition or 4) must also be met even when one has a true belief. One's perceptual faculties must be reliable in such a way that there is a high enough objective probability that the belief will be true, and not merely 50 percent as described in the previous case.

In the next section I present Plantinga's arguments where he argues that if Christian belief is true, then Christian belief is likely to be warranted. Just as it was with perceptual belief where one can hold to one's perceptual beliefs in the basic way without offering an argument, Plantinga will argue that one can hold to Christian belief in the basic way without offering an argument for the truth of Christian belief.[48]

THE EXTENDED A/C MODEL AND PROPER FUNCTION

Plantinga argues that if Christian belief (CE) is true, then Christian belief is likely to be warranted.[49] Call this claim PC. To support PC, he

---

48. Plantinga however does not argue that Christian belief is a *perception* of God or even something like perception. Rather, he argues that Christian belief can have warrant without an argument for the truth of Christian belief in the same way perceptual belief can have warrant without an argument for perceptual belief. One of Plantinga's primary goals is to draw a parallel between a) the warrant for perceptual belief and b) the warrant for Christian belief. This of course is different from arguing that Christian belief is a perception or perceptual in nature. For an argument for religious perception, see Alston, *Perceiving God*.

49. The extended A/C model is strictly speaking not a part of CE. Rather the extended A/C model is one way of seeing that CE is warranted, if in fact CE were to be true.

offers a model on which Christian belief can be warranted. He defines a model, S, as such:

> ... a proposition or state of affairs S is to show *how it could be* that S is true or actual. The model itself will be *another* proposition, one such that it is clear a) that it is possible and b) that if it is *true*, then so is the target proposition. From these two, of course, it follows that the target proposition is possible.[50]

The model plays an essential role for Plantinga's argument in defending PC. Why give a model rather than arguing directly for the truth of Christian belief? We see that according to Plantinga's religious epistemology he is convinced there are no arguments that would show conclusively that Christian belief is in fact true. So there are two purposes for presenting such a model. First, it is to show the possibility of Christian belief by presenting such a model. Next, it is to move from that model to PC. This is a wholly different strategy from arguing that Christian belief indeed *is* warranted or true. One could not construct a model for just any proposition, for example for "square circles" or "married bachelors" since we're dealing in the realm of possibilities here. Plantinga's goal is to defend the conditional conclusion PC rather than a conclusion claiming that Christian belief is true or in fact warranted.[51]

Though Plantinga believes his models are true, he does not argue that the models are true since the models he provides presupposes that certain features of Christian belief are true.[52] So the goal of this model-

---

50. Plantinga, *Warranted Christian Belief*, 168 (Plantinga's emphasis).

51. Consider an example. Although Kurt Gödel was convinced that he had a modal version of the ontological argument for the existence of God that was sound, he never published it. Some believe the reason was that Gödel didn't think it actually established God's existence to those who disagreed. Perhaps Gödel's modal ontological argument was merely something on which God's existence is shown to be possible rather than actual. Like Plantinga, Gödel seems to have accepted the existence of God prior to working on this proof. That is, his version of the ontological argument is not the reason for his coming to accept the proposition that 'God exists' is true. Likewise, Plantinga in offering a model is simply showing what features are necessary for Christian belief to be warranted, if Christian belief is true, on his model. Put another way, one may argue that the premises of Gödel's argument would be accepted only if one already presupposed the existence of God. Perhaps Plantinga's models are doing something similar. See the following for more on Gödel and his version of the modal ontological argument: 1) Anderson, "Some Emendations of Gödel's Ontological Proof," 2) Gödel, "Ontological Proof," 3) Hazen, "On Gödel's Ontological Proof," 4) Sobel, "Gödel's Ontological Proof," and 5) Fitting, *Types, Tableaus, and Gödel's God*.

52. As we shall see in chapter 4, Plantinga claims that this form of argument and ensuing model can be applied to certain other religious belief systems.

centered approach is to show that if one presupposes that Christian belief is true, then the model would show one way that Christian belief could likely be warranted. Plantinga claims there are a range of models on which Christian belief (as he has described) can be warranted. So his model is simply one of many such models where Christian belief is shown to be possible if one presupposes the truth of Christian belief. That is, the primary features of CE may be included in other models that are sufficiently similar to Plantinga's model for CE. Plantinga's main target is the objector to Christian belief who claims that Christian belief is irrational even though he is unable to show that Christian belief is false. Plantinga's goal in offering a model for CE is to counteract such an objector by arguing that one cannot claim Christian belief is irrational, without also showing that Christian belief is in fact false. Plantinga labels his model for Christian belief the 'extended Aquinas/Calvin (AC) model' for warranted Christian belief.[53] If his model is coherent, then he claims that PC is true. Of course this doesn't show that Christian belief is true or that it is in fact warranted.

What are the features of Christian belief? According to Plantinga, CE consists of the central teachings of Christian belief as shown in the "intersection of the great Christian creeds."[54] What Plantinga seems to have in mind here is just the very basic propositions that fall out of the Christian theological statements of faith that unite every sort of Christian, usually this encompasses the two propositions of CE. So by "Christian belief," Plantinga has in mind not a narrow subset of propositions that are specific to Catholicism or Protestantism but something broad that unites most everyone who identifies himself or herself as a Christian. So the purpose of setting up the extended A/C model for Plantinga is not to defend any subset of Christian belief, but just the basic propositions that would unite all those who hold to Christian belief. On this picture then, Christian belief is identical to CE. As I have done throughout this book, Christian belief will be used synonymously with CE.

So now we turn to our main question: what are the primary features of the extended A/C model? First, the beliefs that are generated

---

53. Plantinga, *Warranted Christian Belief*, 241. Before he presents the extended A/C model for Christian belief, Plantinga offers a model he calls the A/C model for theistic belief. My focus will be on the extended A/C model since my concerns are squarely with CE and Plantinga's Christian exclusivism.

54. Ibid., 248.

by the extended A/C model are warranted for Plantinga because they are produced in a way that satisfies the conditions for warrant. They are beliefs that are produced by cognitive faculties functioning properly in an appropriate environment according to a design plan successfully aimed at the production of true beliefs.[55] How is this possible? Basing his ideas on what he finds in Aquinas and Calvin, Plantinga claims that God has enabled in each person a cognitive faculty known as the *sensus divinitatis* (SD) or sense of divinity. The SD can be properly functioning, malfunctioning, or perhaps even damaged. Hence, not everyone is even aware they have an SD. A person however, with a properly functioning SD, can produce warranted religious beliefs if they are in a particular environment according to a design plan that is successfully aimed at the production of true beliefs. Perhaps the right environment may be a particular religious upbringing, someone coming in contact with the right sort of people at the right time, or perhaps even something else.

The production of such beliefs is analogous to other belief producing processes such as perceptual beliefs, in that beliefs produced by the SD are 1) properly basic, and 2) fallible. Plantinga's strategy is to draw a parallel between the production of perceptual beliefs and the production of beliefs generated by the SD, though he makes it clear that the sort of beliefs generated by the SD are not perceptual in nature. The parallel is between the way perceptual beliefs and SD beliefs are generated, rather than in the kind of beliefs they are. Just as perceptual beliefs come from the belief being formed in the appropriate sort of circumstances, SD beliefs are formed in the appropriate sort of circumstances. As was the case with perceptual belief, Plantinga echoes Thomas Reid in claiming that even if one does believe they are being appeared to in such and such way it isn't necessary that one has to believe on any sort of evidential basis for the SD belief to have warrant. SD beliefs, like perceptual beliefs, are held in the basic way. Thus Plantinga claims that "the beliefs constituting faith are typically taken as basic; that is, they are not accepted by way of argument from other propositions."[56] These beliefs can be brought about directly by God via the SD, since the extended A/C model presupposes the existence of God. This of course makes beliefs generated by the SD distinct from beliefs such as memory, perception, and other natu-

---

55. Ibid., 284.
56. Ibid., 250.

ral cognitive processes due to SD beliefs being supernatural in nature.[57] However, beliefs produced by the SD are similar to natural beliefs in that they *can* be warranted if they are produced by properly functioning cognitive faculty according to a design plan aimed at the production of true beliefs.

One of the roles of having an SD is so that beliefs generated by the SD can bring about cognitive renewal such that one is able to see the deliverances of God in God's son Jesus Christ from our sin.[58] Of course this is only what the SD would deliver if in fact Christianity is true. According to Plantinga (and to most that hold to Christian belief), sin has separated humanity from God and prevents us from living a life according to God's design plan—which is the ultimate goal of a person. One of these deliverances is acknowledging propositions such as CE, and doing so gives us a clearer view of the world we live in. Again, the model shows one such possible way that Christian belief *can* be warranted if in fact Christian belief is true.

In summary, the two key primary features of the extended A/C model include the following:[59]

1) The *sensus divinitatis*, a cognitive faculty implanted by God, whose role is to bring about cognitive renewal such that one is able to see the deliverances of God from one's own sin through God's son Jesus Christ in the acknowledging of specifically Christian beliefs such as CE.[60]

2) Beliefs produced by the SD are basic in nature and are not warranted via an appeal to argument but by their basicality.[61]

57. Ibid., 246, 258–29.

58. Ibid., 280–89.

59. Although Plantinga's description of the extended A/C model includes more minor features, I only list the two primary key features of the model since I am only concerned with their impact on Christian exclusivism.

60. It may be that other religions are also warranted in this way if in fact true. Though if that were the case, then it wouldn't strictly speaking be the SD but something else. Plantinga claims that certain other theistic religions in particular may be warranted in the same way via a model that is very analogous to the standard A/C model for theistic belief. I discuss this notion further in chapter 4 and argue that it doesn't pose much of a problem for the extended A/C model and Christian belief (CE).

61. An additional feature is that beliefs generated by the SD are fallible, in much the same way that perceptual beliefs are also fallible. Of course this doesn't show that they are not warranted.

The strategy used by Plantinga is to claim that the extended A/C model shows how it is *possible* that Christian belief can be warranted if Christian belief were true. The model assumes that there is such a being as God and that God created the universe and all its inhabitants. This is precisely why Plantinga claims that "if the fact is there are no good philosophical objections to the model, given the *truth* of Christian belief, then any successful objection to the model will also have to be a successful objection to the truth of Christian belief."[62]

In this chapter I presented 1) Plantinga's arguments for warrant as proper function and 2) the two primary features of the extended A/C model. I have responded to Bonjour's arguments that moderate foundationalist externalist accounts such as Plantinga's proper function as warrant account are unable to account for his Norman case. I argued against this notion, and tried to show that Plantinga's proper function account can explain cases such as Norman's at least as well as any internalist account. This is primarily to motivate the first premise of my main argument, that "if Plantinga's proper function account is a reasonable account of warrant, then rival religious views to CE do not serve as a defeater to Christian belief having warrant." Next, I examined the application of a proper function account of warrant to both perceptual belief and Christian belief. The primary goal of this chapter was to argue that a properly functioning person could reasonably hold to Christian belief even when she has no argument that would convince those who disagree with her about the truth-value of CE.

---

62. Plantinga, *Warranted Christian Belief*, 285. One may ask why is it that Christian belief has to be a part of the model? Why not have the SD faculty itself (without Christian belief) be the model and leave the model neutral among the religious beliefs it might form, in the same way that perception as a faculty is neutral about beliefs supported? This would of course make it much easier on Plantinga. This would presuppose that all religious beliefs are generated by similar faculty. However, it's not clear these particular SD-without-Christian-beliefs would generate non-contradictory beliefs since different religious systems typically have mutually exclusive beliefs. Plantinga does argue for two models, a standard A/C model for theistic belief—which may be in line with the other theistic religions of the world (Islam, Judaism, etc.). The standard A/C model for theistic belief is distinct from the extended A/C model, which is specifically concerned with Christian belief. The standard A/C model for theism is contained within the extended A/C model for Christian belief. Since the goal of Plantinga's project is to argue for CE, his primary concern is with the extended A/C model.

3

Epistemic Disagreement
and the Equal Weight Theory

IN THIS CHAPTER, I turn to the notion of epistemic disagreement.[1] I will argue that the Equal Weight View (EW) is mistaken:

> In cases of peer disagreement, one should give equal weight to the opinion of an epistemic peer and to one's own opinion. An epistemic peer is someone who is alike epistemically in every way given the particular belief in matters of intelligence, honesty, thoroughness, exposure to question/research/data, etc.

I will then argue that PRD (the argument for the problem of religious diversity) and the ensuing claim that CE is not defensible due to its multiple competitors is mistaken because it is essentially a version of the Equal Weight View.

Consider the following cases, both generating much controversy among experts in the particular area:

---

1. There is a burgeoning literature with respect to epistemic disagreement. My goal is not to give complete arguments, but simply point out that it's a reasonable position to challenge the Equal Weight View. There are several other views that are distinct from the Equal Weight View. Although some of what follows may lead to one or more of the following views, my intention is not to endorse any one of them but simply to argue against the Equal Weight View. Some of these other views are: 1) The No Independent Weight View—in at least some cases of peer disagreement, it can be perfectly reasonable to give no weight at all to the opinion of the other party. 2) The Symmetrical No Independent Weight View—in some cases of peer disagreement, both parties to the dispute might be perfectly reasonable even if neither gives any weight at all to the opinion of the other party. 3) Total Evidence View—what it is reasonable to believe depends on both the original, first-order evidence as well as on the higher-order evidence that is afforded by the fact that one's peers believe as they do.

(1) Compatibilism vs. incompatibilism with respect to free will,

(2) and whether a low carbohydrate diet is healthier than a low protein diet when it comes to weight-loss.[2]

Suppose there are two people who disagree on the above issues, let's call them "you" and "I." Suppose you and I are in disagreement about (1). Suppose that you are a trained professional philosopher who has spent your entire career arguing for compatibilism. You have published several books and articles on the topic in peer reviewed journals, and your epistemic peers generally regard you as highly competent in the field. Suppose that I have the exact same credentials and am considered your epistemic peer, yet I have spent my entire philosophical career arguing for incompatibilism. Should the mere fact that an epistemic peer disagrees with you, when we share the same evidence, force you to change your beliefs by retreating into agnosticism or skepticism with respect to the belief? In other words, should one give equal weight to the opinion of an epistemic peer and to one's own opinion?

Initially one would suppose not. After all, if all philosophers endorsed EW this would mean that philosophical debates, such as (1), would never occur. One would always have to give up—to some degree—one's own conclusions and move in the direction of one's peers while expecting one's peers to do the same. However, the compatibilists in (1) are convinced they have the *better* arguments on their side while the incompatibilists are convinced they have the better arguments on their side. Even though both parties have access to the same relevant evidence (the arguments both sides generate), neither is about to give up their beliefs or retreat into agnosticism/skepticism.

Should all compatibilists and incompatibilists arrive at some midway point between their conclusions, such that they retreat into some sort of agnosticism? If EW is correct, this is precisely the course of action that should be taken. Or perhaps at the least, one should lower their confidence in their conclusions because an epistemic peer disagrees. If I am an incompatibilist because I am convinced this is where the evidence is leading me, should I assign an equal weight or probability to the con-

2. Compatibilism is typically the belief that free will and determinism are compatible in that it is possible for one to hold to both without any logical inconsistency. Those who deny this and claim that free will and determinism are not compatible and therefore logically inconsistent are called incompatibilists.

clusions of my opponents? Should they assign equal weight to my views, even though they are convinced their arguments are correct? In what follows, I will argue no. In arguing no (as we shall see), I will not be arguing for a specific view applicable to all cases of epistemic disagreement. I will simply argue that EW is mistaken, and that the arguments for PRD presuppose EW.

A few clarifications are in order. Epistemic disagreement falls squarely under the category of normative questions. The primary concern is how these questions of disagreement should affect our beliefs. Answering these questions should tell us what to do in a given situation should one find themselves in a similar situation. Although some may want to argue that the reason or best explanation for why there is so much disagreement about such matters is that there are no facts of the matter, if there are no facts of the matter then there are no facts upon which one can agree or disagree on.[3] Hence, I want to rule out any non-factual position that claims there are no *facts of the matter* with regard to the disputed question. Though there are interesting questions worth pursuing with regards to this non-factualist thesis, I will not pursue them. As was stated in the first chapter, I will assume that CE_1 and CE_2 are propositions and can in principle in some possible world be confirmed as true or false. Finally, my concern will be squarely upon those for whom we have no discernible epistemic advantage, an epistemic peer. So our case is quite different from cases as such:

1. Someone who is an epistemic peer in terms of intelligence, training, and the like but who has not been exposed to the questions in the same manner.

2. Someone who has been exposed to the pertinent questions but is not an epistemic peer in terms of intelligence, training, etc.

In the case of PRD, unlike 1 and 2 above, we are concerned with someone who is an epistemic peer not only with respect to intelligence and training, but also exposure to the pertinent questions surrounding the particular area of disagreement.

---

3. See Mackie, *Ethics*, for an example of non-factualism.

EPISTEMIC DISAGREEMENT: KELLY

Thomas Kelly argues that disagreement, even by an epistemic peer, does not provide a good reason to retreat into agnosticism or skepticism, provided the view was carefully scrutinized and all the available relevant evidence and arguments were examined.[4] He argues further that the mere fact that an epistemic peer exists who has scrutinized the question in the same manner that I have and come to a different conclusion does not undermine the rationality of my own particular position. Retaining one's original view, even in the face of epistemic disagreement, may be the required rational response in such a situation. This position of course, goes directly against EW.

Kelly defines an epistemic peer as such:

(i)   They are equals with respect to their familiarity with the evidence and arguments which bear on that question, and

(ii) they are equals with respect to general epistemic virtues such as intelligence, thoughtfulness, and freedom from bias.[5]

The difficulty in assessing whether someone is an epistemic peer, outside of perhaps a mathematical context, is that the standards are typically context-sensitive. So even if two people are epistemic equals, whether they are in fact epistemic peers on the particular issue depends on the standards for epistemic peerhood within that particular context.[6] If one pushes this distinction even further, Kelly claims that perhaps no two individuals are in fact epistemic peers with exact precision. Still, our intuitions seem to side on the notion of the existence of epistemic peers and our precision tends to be liberal enough to be able to identify when two people are such with respect to a given issue.

A common argument given in favor of EW is as follows:

1) It is unreasonable to hold to one's views in the face of disagreement since one would need some positive reason to privilege one's views over one's opponents.

---

4. Kelly, "Epistemic Significance of Disagreement."

5. Ibid., 10.

6. Whether two individuals are the "same height" will depend on the precision of the standards used. David Lewis has a discussion of such issues of context sensitivity in Lewis, "Scorekeeping in a Language Game."

2) No such reason is available since the disagreeing parties are epistemic peers and have access to the same evidence.

3) Therefore, one should give equal weight to the opinion of an epistemic peer and to one's own opinion in cases of epistemic disagreement.

Kelly disputes this via an appeal to symmetry. Consider again our disagreeing epistemic peers, "you" and "I," with respect to some issue H. I come to believe H as a result of examining the evidence while you come to believe ~H while examining the same issue.[7] This seems to be a case of perfect symmetry, after all I do not claim to be smarter or in possession of some key argument that you lack access to. We are both aware of the other's arguments. Given this, how could I not give your view equal weight to my own?

At first glance the most rational thing to do seems to be to head towards EW. From a third party's perspective, it seems that when two equally competent epistemic peers disagree one should give equal weight to both views. However, it doesn't follow from this that we have perfect symmetry. Consider the perspective of "I." From my perspective, you have misjudged the force of the evidence. Of course from my perspective, I can claim that this particular difference is a relevant difference in showing that things are not perfectly symmetrical. Of course one may ask whether this particular assessment, that you have misjudged the evidence, is consistent with you and I being regarded as epistemic peers. Kelly answers yes. Two chess players of equal skill do not always play to a draw, sometimes one of the players wins decisively even though both are equal in their skill. Likewise it is not always the case that two epistemic peers judge the force of the evidence correctly at the same time on all occasions.

The point is that on *this particular occasion*, I have done a better job than you in weighing the evidence and the competing considerations. One need not assume that I will always do a better job. However there is a problem. Since both you and I are epistemically fallible, wouldn't you reason in much the same manner and claim that it is I and not you that has misjudged the evidence? Kelly claims that this doesn't show that I am irrational for holding on to H since the rationality of the parties

---

7. Again, the symbol ~ is the negation symbol.

depends on who *in fact* has correctly evaluated the evidence. Kelly says of this that:

> ... the rationality of one's believing as one does is not threatened by the fact that there are those who believe otherwise. Rather, any threat to the rationality of one's believing as one does depends on whether those who believe otherwise have good reasons for believing as they do—reasons that one has failed to accurately appreciate in arriving at one's own view.[8]

Kelly claims that since one is not privy to a God's-eye view of the epistemic situation, so long as the conditions of epistemic peerness are met and one has judged the force of the evidence correctly, one does not believe irrationally in holding to H even if you hold to ~H based on the same evidence. On this view, the normative claim of EW is false, since the only thing that would move one to change their beliefs is the force of the arguments and not the existence of an epistemic peer who disagrees. Kelly offers two main arguments for this conclusion.

The first argument centers on cases such as Newcomb's Paradox.[9] In Newcomb's Paradox, there are only two choices one can make: 1) choose

---

8. Kelly, "Epistemic Significance of Disagreement," 17.

9. Consider the following definition of Newcomb's Paradox from Wikipedia: "A person is playing a game operated by the Predictor, an entity somehow presented as being exceptionally skilled at predicting people's actions. The exact nature of the Predictor varies between retellings of the paradox. Some assume that the character always has a reputation for being completely infallible and incapable of error. The Predictor can be presented as a psychic, as a super intelligent alien, as a deity, etc. However, the original discussion by Nozick says only that the Predictor's predictions are "almost certainly" correct, and also specifies that "what you actually decide to do is not part of the explanation of why he made the prediction he made." With this original version of the problem, some of the discussion below is inapplicable. The player of the game is presented with two opaque boxes, labeled A and B. The player is permitted to take the contents of both boxes, or just of box B. (The option of taking only box A is ignored, for reasons soon to be obvious.) Box A contains $1,000. The contents of box B, however, are determined as follows: At some point before the start of the game, the Predictor makes a prediction as to whether the player of the game will take just box B, or both boxes. If the Predictor predicts that both boxes will be taken, then box B will contain nothing. If the Predictor predicts that only box B will be taken, then box B will contain $1,000,000. By the time the game begins, and the player is called upon to choose which boxes to take, the prediction has already been made, and the contents of box B have already been determined. That is, box B contains either $0 or $1,000,000 before the game begins, and once the game begins even the Predictor is powerless to change the contents of the boxes. Before the game begins, the player is aware of all the rules of the game, including the two possible contents of box B, the fact that its contents are based on the Predictor's predic-

two boxes—A and B, or 2) just one box—B. The former are known as Two-boxers while the latter are known as One-boxers. Nozick says of Newcomb's Paradox that:

> I have put this problem to a large number of people...To almost everyone it is perfectly clear and obvious what should be done. The difficulty is that these people seem to divide almost evenly on the problem, with large numbers thinking that the opposing half is just being silly.[10]

Suppose that the members of the philosophical community in our world who have seriously thought about Newcomb's Paradox and are familiar with the relevant literature on both sides are evenly divided between Two-boxers and One-boxers. Suppose also that the philosophers who are divided on this issue are epistemic peers in the way described previously.[11] So let this evenly divided scenario be our current world, W_1.[12]

tion, and knowledge of the Predictor's infallibility. The only information withheld from the player is what prediction the Predictor made, and thus what the contents of box B are. *The problem is called a paradox* because two strategies that both sound intuitively logical give conflicting answers to the question of what choice maximizes the player's payout. *The first strategy* argues that, regardless of what prediction the Predictor has made, taking both boxes yields more money. That is, if the prediction is for both A and B to be taken, then the player's decision becomes a matter of choosing between $1,000 (by taking A and B) and $0 (by taking just B), in which case taking both boxes is obviously preferable. But, even if the prediction is for the player to take only B, then taking both boxes yields $1,001,000, and taking only B yields only $1,000,000—the difference is comparatively slight in the latter case, but taking both boxes is still better, regardless of which prediction has been made. *The second strategy* suggests taking only B. By this strategy, we can ignore the possibilities that return $0 and $1,001,000, as they both require that the Predictor has made an incorrect prediction, and the problem states that the Predictor cannot be wrong. Thus, the choice becomes whether to receive $1,000 (both boxes) or to receive $1,000,000 (only box B)—so taking only box B is better."

10. Nozick, "Newcomb's Problem and Two principles of Choice."

11. Kelly, "The Epistemic Significance of Disagreement," 19. Kelly claims that in the nearly four decades of debate on Newcomb's paradox, that there has been a significant shift in the original distribution in favor of Two-Boxing. However, for the purposes of epistemic disagreement as Kelly notes, it matters not which position is preferred. We can consider this issue as having taken place in 1969 where there was a fairly even divide.

12. World here refers to logically possible worlds or logically possible states of affairs. For example, in the 2008 presidential election in the USA it was logically possible for John McCain to have won the presidency over Barack Obama. Even though Obama won the election, there is nothing illogical about John McCain winning the presidency. However, there are no worlds that contain married bachelors or square circles since these are not logically possible.

Consider a few possible worlds where there is consensus on New-comb's Paradox such that only Two-boxers exist:

W_2 There is an ingenious argument that convinces all of the One-boxers that they have been in error.

W_3 An evil tyrant rids the world of all the One-boxer philosophers by killing them all. (The mere absence of disagreement though is of no epistemic significance.)

W_4 There is no disagreement about Newcomb's Paradox. There is no ingenious argument or evil tyrant. The only known arguments are the ones we posses in W_1. All the philosophers in W_4 who have studied Newcomb's paradox have come to their position for Two-boxing based on the same arguments we have in W_1.

The only difference then, between W_1 and W_2—W_4 is that in the latter worlds *all* the living philosophers who have given Newcomb's Paradox serious thought are convinced by the arguments for Two-boxing, the same arguments that we possess in world W_1. Suppose further that in W_4 there is no other explanation for this phenomenon, since it is a world exactly like ours except for the aforementioned point. Hence, W_2, W_3, and W_4, has only Two-boxers though the philosophers of each world have different reasons—more specifically different arguments—for why they are Two-boxers.

Now imagine there is a very bright philosophy student who sets out to study Newcomb's Paradox. She studies the arguments that favor both One-boxing and Two-boxing and exposes herself to all the relevant literature that is available in our world W_1. She finds that approximately half the philosophers are One-boxers, while the other half are Two-boxers. After exposing herself to all the relevant literature, she resolves to make up her mind on her own by focusing solely on the arguments surrounding Newcomb's Paradox. She comes to her conclusion after examining all the arguments and concludes that One-boxing is correct. What would we expect her reaction to be in the other possible worlds?

In W_2, she probably would be convinced by the ingenious argument for Two-boxing in much the same way the other philosophers were convinced. In W_3, the mere fact that there exists only Two-boxers shouldn't do much to sway her philosophically (though it may sway her psychologically) since she has access to the same arguments in our world W_1 and W_3. In W_4 should she take a different view of Newcomb's Paradox versus W_1 despite the fact that her decision would be based on the *exact same arguments* in both worlds? This seems to be an extremely dubious line of thinking. She would not move her position towards Two-boxing simply because there were no One-boxers, since she had considered all the arguments that swayed the Two-boxers in W_4 to become Two-boxers. The mere fact that others disagree should not sway her since she had already spent time in the relevant literature and considered all the arguments for both One-boxing and Two-boxing before coming to her conclusion. Of course this seems to be precisely the position that EW endorses.

Consider a parallel to arguments for radical skepticism and the way epistemologists have treated arguments for radical skepticism. One would be hard pressed to find any contemporary philosopher who is a genuine skeptic about other minds. Consider such a skeptic, someone who is unsure whether other minds actually exist. Though there may exist significant numbers of such skeptics, it's hard to imagine someone who would take this view seriously.[13] One main reason is the difficulty in *psychologically* becoming a skeptic. How does one start? Did they get these ideas in a vacuum apart from society? These are difficult questions to answer. Regardless of the existence of such skeptics, given the vast literature in epistemology on refuting the skeptic, one can prudently claim that very few philosophers *actually* believe there is some sound argument for skepticism about other minds. Though some philosophers have defended skeptical arguments in showing that certain objections to them are weak or misguided or don't believe that we have a really good objection to these skeptical arguments, this is still weaker than offering an argument that has as its conclusion: *I cannot know whether there is another mind besides my own.* In this last sense of actually offering an

---

13. Russell, *Human Knowledge: Its Scope and Limits*, 180. Bertrand Russell once dabbled with philosophical solipsism, the view that there were no other minds besides one's own. Christine Ladd Franklin wrote to Russell and told him that she agreed with him and was swayed by his arguments—she too was a solipsist. Of course Russell abandoned solipsism after this correspondence. He was convinced to give up his solipsism even though he had not encountered an argument that had as its conclusion: solipsism is false.

argument for skepticism, Kelly claims there have been very few genuine skeptics about other minds.[14]

We can of course imagine a world where the philosophical community is evenly divided among those that are convinced the arguments for skepticism of the mind are correct and those that demur, in much the same way it was once divided for Newcomb's Paradox. The key here then is that the case for or against skepticism stands or falls on the force of the arguments surrounding skepticism and not the contingent and empirical facts that fall out, including the existence of actual skeptics. Likewise, the arguments for One-boxing or Two-boxing in Newcomb's Paradox stand or fall on the actual arguments surrounding Newcomb's Paradox and not the contingent and empirical facts that fall out of the issue (i.e., the actual existence of One-boxers or Two-boxers). If this thesis is true, the existence of those who disagree may not be sufficient as a reason for you to give up your beliefs on an issue of epistemic disagreement. The crucial factor is the argument for a particular position, and the argument is why someone would hold their ground or change their position with respect to a particular disagreement. So one should *not* always give equal weight to the opinion of an epistemic peer and to one's own opinion since what is key is the actual argument or evidence at hand. Hence, EW is mistaken.

The second key argument for Kelly centers on viewing *one's peers* as higher-order evidence, which is distinct from viewing *their arguments* as higher-order evidence. We typically recognize that those who are reasonable respond a particular way to their evidence in terms of drawing the right sort of inferences and the like, though even reasonable people make mistakes and are not infallible. The fact that a reasonable individual responds to evidence in a particular way is itself another type of evidence: it is evidence about her evidence. So a reasonable person believing H based on evidence E is itself some evidence that it is reasonable to believe H based on E. This is *higher order* evidence, namely evidence about the character of her first-order evidence. Of course higher order evidence is not conclusive (like most other evidence). Just because a reasonable person believes H based on E does not mean that it is always

14. Kelly, "The Epistemic Significance of Disagreement," 22. Kelly also claims this in footnote 19: "The relatively recent advent of skeptic-friendly varieties of contextualism might cause some difficulties for this (admittedly rough) construal of what counts as 'genuine skepticism.' But not, I think, in a way that materially affects the point at issue."

reasonable to believe H based on E nor does it mean that we should always believe H based on E simply because a reasonable person does.

Suppose that E again is the total evidence with respect to some proposition H. Consider the following: E is good evidence that H is true. In the aforementioned view of viewing one's peers as higher-order evidence, if one discovers that a reasonable person believes H because of E then one should treat this discovery as additional confirming evidence for H. Likewise, if a reasonable person rejects H because of E then one should also treat this discovery as additional evidence against H. Should I now add the former and latter as additional evidence (either confirming or disconfirming) for H in addition to E when considering H? Kelly argues no.

Suppose I have not yet made up my mind about H and am in the process of deliberating whether to accept or reject H based on E. Suppose further that I find out that you accept H based on E. If I treat this fact as an additional piece of evidence for the truth of H, I will not only list E as a reason for my acceptance of H but also the fact that you (a reasonable person) accept H based on E. However, when you list why you believe that H is true, you only list E since the fact that you believe as you do is the result of your assessment of E with respect to H. Your confidence in H is based solely on E and not because you yourself also accept H on the basis of E. So we have the following:

a)   You accept H because of 1) E.

b)   I accept H because of 1) E and 2) your acceptance of H because of E.

This is an odd result since, on this view, that would mean I have additional evidence that you lack, namely 2) your acceptance of H because of E. It would be something entirely different if I lacked access to E and were to accept H based on you accepting H. However, we are dealing with a case of epistemic disagreement where we both have the same access to E. Given this, it would be very odd to claim that I'm in a better epistemic position than you are with respect to H since I have an additional piece of evidence, namely 2) your acceptance of H because of E, that you lack. At the very least, Kelly claims, there is an awkwardness from me giving additional weight to your belief that H is true when I have already taken into account all that your belief in H is based on.

Kelly concedes that "issues about how one's higher-order evidence does (or does not) interact with one's first-order evidence when that first-order evidence is itself available are, I think, extremely complicated" and thus the previous argument is by no means conclusive.[15] Even if we do treat the higher-order evidence of our epistemic peers as additional evidence, it still does not follow that one should be skeptical or agnostic to the disagreement.

Consider another example. Let us suppose again that E is our total evidence with respect to H at time t_0. Let us further suppose that each of us is ignorant of the others existence at t_0. Suppose also that E rationalizes the belief that H, and that you form the reasonable belief H at t_1 an instant after t_0. However, I misjudge E and take up the unreasonable belief that ~H at t_1. So at time t_1 we have:

You	hold the reasonable belief that H based on E
I	hold the unreasonable belief that ~H based on E

The only asymmetry with respect to the epistemic status of our beliefs is that E does in fact support H, and does not support ~H. Now, suppose at t_2 we become aware of our disagreement. So on the view that our peers are higher-order evidence, our total evidence E for both parties with respect to H is different at t_2 from t_1. What is our total evidence?

$E(t_1) =$ (i)   the original first order evidence E

　　　　　　+

　　　　(ii)   your belief H on the basis of E

vs.

$E(t_2) =$ (i)   the original first order evidence E

　　　　　　+

　　　　(ii)   your belief H on the basis of E

　　　　　　+

　　　　(iii)   my belief ~H on the basis of E

Kelly argues here that there is no reason to think that (ii) your belief H at t_1 is unreasonable given $E(t_2)$ since it was reasonable at $E(t_1)$, which was the moment you were unaware of our disagreement. Even if we give equal weight to (i), (ii), and (iii), it is still more probable that H than

15. Ibid., 27.

~H since we have two pieces of evidence for H (i) and (ii) versus just one piece of evidence for ~H (iii). Our evidence E does not vanish or become irrelevant even if we learn of our disagreement, rather it continues to play an important role as a subset of E(t$_2$). The key in both t$_1$ and t$_2$, is (i) the original first order E. In this regard then, Kelly claims that even if we treat the higher order evidence of the beliefs of one's peers as evidence on a particular disputed thesis, it does not follow from this alone that agnosticism or suspension of judgment or skepticism is the correct response.[16] The mere existence of those who dissent to H does very little to change E, just as "a genuine counterexample to a modal claim is no stronger in virtue of being an actual, empirically discovered counterexample."[17]

TWO ADDITIONAL CASES

Consider the following two additional cases:

Case One:
You and your identical twin have been going out to eat at restaurants together for many years. Both of you are mathematicians and pride yourselves on doing accurate and quick calculations of the bill including tax and tip. Though you agree and come up with the same numbers the majority of the time, occasionally you disagree. In all of the cases where you have disagreed, a quick second mental calculation reveals that one of you was wrong. Assume there has been an even number of such cases so that you have been wrong as much as your twin has. Consider a case where after such a calculation, you disagree on the number on the bill: you think it's $99 while your twin claims it's $98. Both of you quickly do the calculation in your head again, and come up with the same result: you claim it's $99 while your twin claims it's $98.

Case Two:
Suppose you are the only philosopher in an isolated country where there is no access to any other philosophers in the world. Suppose you have been working on issues concerning free will. You consider what you believe to be the best arguments for and against the compatibility of free will and determinism. Based on your extensive research, you come to the conclusion that compatibilism is true with respect to free will. Suppose

16. Ibid., 29.
17. Ibid., 31.

further that your country finally gains access to other philosophers and you are exposed to philosophers who are incompatibilists. As you are reading the incompatibilist arguments of these philosophers, you realize that they are the exact same arguments that you had considered when coming to your position. However, this time they are endorsed by actual living philosophers rather than just an opponent you came up with in your mind.

In both cases we have conditions that are similar to the Newcomb's Paradox case: 1) an epistemic peer or peers who disagree, and 2) access to similar evidence. This is where the similarity ends. Case One is significantly different from Case Two. In Case One the disagreement can be settled quickly by consulting an additional piece of evidence, a calculator, that was unavailable at the time. Unlike Case One, in Case Two no additional evidence is available apart from the arguments that both parties to the disagreement have access to.

Given the epistemic disagreement in Case Two, one can either hold on to the belief, give up the belief, or retreat into agnosticism/skepticism with respect to the belief. What should be the response once our lonely philosopher finds out that there are *actual* (vs. imaginary) people who endorse arguments that he has already considered?

Assume the time at which you find out that there actually exist philosophers who endorse incompatibilism is T_1. Suppose T_0 is the time immediately preceding this moment. Let E again be the evidence you possess, which are the arguments for and against compatibilism. Let H be your belief, which here is that compatibilism is true and let ~H be the belief that compatibilism is false or incompatibilism is true. So we have T_0 vs. T_1:

$T_0 =$ (i)   the original first order evidence E

+

(ii)   your belief H on the basis of E

vs.

$T_1 =$ (i)   the original first order evidence E

+

(ii)   your belief H on the basis of E

+

(iii)   the existence of other philosophers who believe ~H on the basis of E as higher order evidence

The only difference between T_0 and T_1 is (iii). The key question now is, does the addition of (iii) give one an additional reason to change one's belief regarding H such that one either gives up H or retreats into agnosticism or skepticism?

Clearly not. First of all, Case Two is set up so that our lonely philosopher is aware of all the arguments for and against compatibilism. He has already thought of all the relevant arguments for H and ~H and still holds to H. The only thing that is added in (iii) is that there are actual philosophers who endorse ~H based on arguments that our lonely philosopher has already considered. If the only difference is (iii), is this sufficient for our lonely philosopher to give up H? Clearly not since our lonely philosopher has already considered all the relevant arguments that are endorsed by these actual living philosophers who hold to ~H.

Even if, again, we give equal weight to (i), (ii), and (iii), it is still not more probable that we should change our belief regarding H since we now have two bits of evidence for H [(i) and (ii)] vs. only one for ~H [(iii)]. As was noted earlier, our evidence does not vanish or become irrelevant simply because we learn that others disagree or that there exists a live person who disagrees. So even if we treat the higher order evidence of one's epistemic peers as evidence with respect to a particular proposition H it does not follow from this that giving up the belief or retreating into agnosticism/skepticism is the correct response. The mere existence of those who dissent to H then, is not sufficient as a reason for one to change one's position.[18]

THE EQUAL WEIGHT THEORY

There is something unsettling about this view as we have seen in both my two cases and Kelly's Newcomb's paradox example in concluding that the mere existence of epistemic peers who disagree is not sufficient as a reason for one to give up one's belief or retreat into skepticism/agnosticism. Let us call this view Z. Assume Z is correct. If Z is correct, then the mere existence of epistemic peers who disagree with Z and endorse ~Z is not sufficient as a reason to give up Z. What is required in this situation is a good argument against Z. So Z has a sense of self-coherency. However,

---

18. There may be psychological reasons for one to lower one's confidence in a particular belief. Still this does nothing to affect the rationality of whether one should give up one's belief or change one's belief simply because there are others who dissent, which is the crux of this issue.

this claim is a bit *psychologically* unsettling. After all, I am no different than anyone else and there seem to be many psychological studies that suggest that humans are highly disposed to being influenced by the views of others. Of course it is an entirely different thing to be affected psychologically as opposed to philosophically.

EW on the other hand does not have the same sense of self-coherency. Consider this common argument given on behalf of EW:

1. Two epistemic peers can come to contradicting conclusions based on the same evidence.

2. Given 1, one should give equal weight to the opinion of an epistemic peer and to one's own opinion.

3. Given 2, one should either give up the concluding belief in question or retreat into agnosticism/skepticism.

This argument for EW contradicts Z. However, if Z is true then EW is on shaky ground. I have argued that Z is true and that EW is on shaky ground. There is however an even more general charge of incoherency against EW.

Suppose there exists a large community of philosophers who endorse EW in one of its relevant forms, and an equally large number of philosophers who reject EW. Assume all parties involved are epistemic peers. They all have access to the same evidence, and both parties are familiar with the arguments of the other party involved. Let E again be the evidence (arguments of both parties involved, etc.) for EW.

1. Some philosophers affirm EW based on E.

2. Some philosophers reject EW based on E.

3. The parties in 1 and 2 are epistemic peers.

4. If EW is true, according to EW the philosophers in 1 should give equal weight to the opinion of the epistemic peers in 2.

5. If the philosophers in 1 give equal weight to the opinion of the epistemic peers in 2, they should give up the belief that EW is true or retreat into agnosticism/skepticism with respect to EW.

Clearly, 5 conflicts with 1, hence the incoherency charge. If EW were true, given the above argument, then all those who affirm EW would have to give up EW based on EW—which is clearly incoherent.

Brian Weatherson has a somewhat similar take on the incoherency and inconsistency of EW.[19] Consider the following questions Q1–Q4:

(Q1) Is EW true?

Assume there are two participants and both of them disagree. One says yes, the other says no. We now have a case of disagreement, which leads to:

(Q2) What is the right reaction to the disagreement over Q1?

A proponent of EW may answer by claiming that the probability for EW should be 0.5, a halfway point between giving up the belief and full acceptance. Of course the opponents of EW disagree and claim there is no reason to move the probability any greater than 0. So we have another case of disagreement, which leads to another question:

(Q3) What is the right reaction to the disagreement over Q2?

Assuming EW is true, we should probably split the difference over the two parties again. So the proponents of EW should assign a probability to EW that is halfway between their probability of 0.5 and their opponent's probability of 0. Hence the current probability would be 0.25. However the opponents of EW disagree again, and claim (again) there is no reason to move the probability any greater than 0. So we yet have another case of disagreement, which leads to another question:

(Q4) What is the right reaction to the disagreement over Q3?

This of course could go on ad infinitum. According to Weatherson, "the only 'stable point' in the sequence is when we assign a credence of 0 to EW."[20] This is because the proponents of EW will assign 0.5, while the opponents will assign 0 to EW. Of course if we do assign 0 to EW, then Weatherson (correctly) points out that the opponents of EW are correct and EW must be given up.

Can EW be salvaged? Perhaps one way would be to claim that EW is true, but set the standards for epistemic peerhood really high. On this picture the proponents of EW can claim that those who disagree with them are not real epistemic peers. Of course to really figure out whether

19. Weatherson, "Disagreeing about Disagreement."
20. Ibid.

someone is an epistemic peer is no small feat. One may have to assess academic transcripts, pour over the peer reviewed journal articles of those in question, assess the number of citations in other peer reviewed journal articles, come up with some sort of interview process to determine whether two people really are epistemic peers, and so on. This of course is absurd. However if EW is true, how can epistemic peerhood be realistically determined so that one can move in the direction of their epistemic peers with respect to EW? One not only has the problem of how to determine the precise standard of epistemic peerhood, but also how to determine whether someone meets that standard. So EW doesn't seem to bode too well in terms of an epistemological theory that's normative in nature, it would be quite difficult or perhaps impossible to actually determine epistemic peerhood to figure out how to apply EW. There is another problem that creeps up if the proponents of EW claim that those who disagree with them are not real epistemic peers. The opponents of EW would disagree and claim they *are* in fact real epistemic peers. Of course then we'd have yet another disagreement, and if we apply EW we end up in the same situation as Weatherson and I have adumbrated earlier. EW seems quite difficult to salvage in terms of its coherency.

THE PROBLEM OF RELIGIOUS DIVERSITY AND THE EQUAL WEIGHT THEORY

How does this affect CE? Is religious disagreement qualitatively different from other types of epistemic disagreement? As two distinct propositions CE_1 and CE_2, CE is not different from any other proposition with respect to having a truth-value. Both CE_1 and CE_2 can be shown as false if certain conditions are met. For CE_1, if someone could show that God does not exist or that metaphysical naturalism is true then CE_1 can be shown to be false. CE_2 can be shown to be false either by falsifying CE_1, or showing that human beings do not require salvation, etc. So in this propositional sense, the issues surrounding CE are no different from any other issue concerning epistemic disagreement. There are two groups of epistemic peers, those advocating CE and those rejecting CE, who have access to the same relevant arguments. These arguments could include natural theological arguments for and against the existence of God, Reformed Epistemological arguments, arguments against Reformed Epistemological arguments, etc. One group based on their evidence—

which includes all the relevant arguments surrounding CE—claims that CE is warranted if true. The other group based on their evidence—which also includes all the relevant arguments surrounding CE—claims that CE is unwarranted and unjustified. The parties are epistemic peers. Of course, the Christian exclusivist will not think that she is on epistemic par with such a person even when she cannot provide a conclusive argument for her Christian belief, she will think that she is epistemically privileged with respect to this belief. The Christian Exclusivist will not think that those who reject CE are her epistemic peers with respect to CE. Perhaps she may think that their SD is damaged or broken. Either way, the Christian exclusivist will consider herself epistemically privileged with respect to CE. This is no problem on Z of course.

Consider the argument for the Problem of Religious Diversity (PRD) again:

1. There are a large variety of mutually exclusive religious propositions held by a large variety of religious believers and non-believers.

2. The believers and non-believers in premise 1 are epistemic peers, people who are alike epistemically in every way given the particular belief in matters of intelligence, honesty, thoroughness, exposure to question/research/data, etc.

3. One should give equal weight to all of the religious propositions in premise 1 because they come from epistemic peers.

4. Given 3, these mutually exclusive religious propositions serve as defeaters for one another.

5. Therefore, it is not tenable to hold to any one particular religious proposition in any exclusive sense.

6. Therefore, any form of religious exclusivism is unwarranted.

The key connection between PRD and EW is premise 3—one should give equal weight to all religious propositions that are generated by epistemic peers. If premise 3 were true, this would seemingly nullify any sort of religious exclusivism, including CE, since any exclusivist would claim that one should *not* give equal weight to all religious propositions. Of course if EW is true, then we should equally accept the views of both a) those that accept premise 3 as true and b) those that reject premise 3 as false. This of course is incoherent. If EW were false, however, then

premise 3 is also false since one need not give equal weight to all religious propositions that are generated by epistemic peers. So premise
3, like EW, is incoherent and thus one need not give equal weight to
all religious propositions or beliefs simply because they come from an
epistemic peer.

The religious exclusivist would also deny premise 2. The religious
exclusivist claims privileged access to God (or the divine or ultimate
reality, etc.) based on religious experience, the extended A/C model and
the SD, or possibly something else.[21] The endorser of PRD will have to
produce an additional non-question begging argument that shows that
all parties in question are in fact epistemic peers with respect to access
to God (or the divine or ultimate reality, etc.). The exclusivist will surely
not accept premise 2 without an argument since she would be convinced
that she is privileged epistemically, and if the endorser of PRD also endorses EW then this too is yet another disagreement. Given this, premise
2—like premise 3—is also problematic.

PRD is unsound because it depends on EW. The claim that CE is
not defensible due to its multiple competitors as construed via EW is
also mistaken. There is however another concern that originates from
PRD in premise 1. Even if one does not give equal weight to all religious
propositions or beliefs simply because they come from epistemic peers,
there are multiple competing religious beliefs in existence. Won't these
multiple mutually exclusive religious beliefs serve as defeaters for one
another given that one cannot show all the other competing religious
beliefs as false? It is this issue that I will turn to in the next chapter.

---

21. Whether the exclusivist is in fact privileged with respect to access to God is an
open question, but this is a different question from whether premise 2 is true.

4

The Great Pumpkin Objection

IN THIS CHAPTER I will consider the nature of defeaters and discuss what I believe to be the most significant objection to Plantinga's Reformed Epistemological defense of Christian exclusivism.

THE NATURE OF DEFEATERS

What is a defeater? Consider the following example given by Plantinga. You see what seems to you to be a sheep in a field at a hundred yards away from your present position. You form the belief there is a sheep in the field. Suppose you then meet the owner of the field, who tells you he has no sheep in his field but that he owns a dog that may be mistaken for a sheep at approximately one hundred yards away. In the absence of some special circumstances, one now has a defeater for their original belief that one saw a sheep in the field. This is a *rebutting* defeater—a defeater where what one learns (i.e., there are no sheep in the field) is inconsistent with the original (and now defeated) belief.

Consider another type of defeater, an *undercutting* defeater. This is an example given by John Pollock. Imagine that you enter a factory and see on an assembly line, a number of widgets that all look red. You form the belief that the widgets are red. Suppose then the superintendent enters and tells you that the widgets are illuminated with a red infrared light so that hairline cracks can be detected in them that would not normally show up. All the widgets look red, regardless of their color. One has a defeater for their original belief that the widgets are red. It may be true that the particular widget one is looking at is red, but one does not have knowledge in this case that the widget is red since the red infrared light would illuminate all of the widgets as red. In an undercutting defeater one does not learn something incompatible with the original belief (as

66

in a *rebutting* defeater), rather one learns something that undercuts one's grounds or reasons for thinking the widget was red. If they are rebutting or undercutting defeaters then they are reasons for accepting a belief incompatible with *p*. Plantinga says of this that "acquiring a defeater for a belief puts you in a position in which you can't rationally continue to hold the belief."[1] The two aforementioned defeaters are rationality defeaters. If one acquires an undercutting or a rebutting defeater *p* for a belief *q*, then one cannot rationally continue to hold to belief *q*. Put another way, a defeater can generally be seen as any good reason for giving up belief *p*.

Another type of defeater is a warrant defeater. Warrant is the quality or quantity that when added to true belief yields knowledge. As we have seen in chapter 2, warrant is not necessarily synonymous with justification though some philosophers equate warrant with justification. In Carl Ginet's now famous fake barn example, one is driving through Wisconsin in barn country and one seems to see plenty of barns in the surrounding landscape. One stops to look at a particular barn, and thinks to oneself "there is a barn." Unbeknownst to you, the natives of Wisconsin have put up many clever looking fake barns in the area so that they are indistinguishable from real barns. The particular barn you are looking at, however, is a real barn and not a fake one. Still, one would claim here that one does not have knowledge that one is looking at a real barn. The presence of these fake barns is a warrant defeater for you since the mere fact that there are plenty of fake barns around would defeat one's belief that there is a real barn in front of you. However, this does not mean that it is irrational for you to believe there is a barn in front of you. There is nothing irrational about holding the belief that there is a real barn given one's circumstances. After all, you are unaware of the fact that there are real looking fake barns around and you happen to be looking at a real barn even though you may not be warranted in that belief.

A defeater for someone is relative to the rest of their noetic structure and is dependent on what one already knows and believes. A defeater *p* for belief *q* is not solely dependent upon my current experience, rather the dependency also hinges on what else I believe and how firmly I hold those other beliefs. Let us return to the aforementioned sheep example again. Suppose, the owner of the field is a friend of yours and you happen to know he's a jokester. He often likes to tell people there are

1. Plantinga, *Warranted Christian Belief*, 359.

no sheep in his field when, in fact, there are sheep present. If I do not consider the owner trustworthy in such matters, then his testimony will not count as a defeater for having seen a sheep. Or perhaps I am seeing a sheep with powerful binoculars and can identify clearly that it is a sheep, even though I know my friend is a jokester and may lie to me about there being any sheep present. For *p* to qualify as a defeater for my sheep belief it is not merely my current experience that comes into play, but other things I know and believe must also be taken into consideration.

Consider two people who have the same belief *p*, such that *p* constitutes a defeater for belief *q* that I hold but not for you. Assume we both believe that Arizona State University was established in 1885, but only you happen to know that the current guidebook for Arizona State University lists the establishment of the school incorrectly as 1890. We both pick up a copy of the guidebook and see that it contains the mistaken date as 1890. Given my noetic structure and the corresponding background beliefs (which includes the belief that guidebooks are accurate and reliable), I now have a defeater for my belief that the university was established in 1885. You, however, know via other sources that the listing of 1890 in the guidebook was a mistake and hence you do not have a defeater for your belief. Whereas I now have a reason to reject the belief that the university was established in 1885, you do not since you already know the guidebook lists this in error. So in such a case we see that a defeater can be relative to a particular noetic structure at a particular point in time such that a belief *p* can be a defeater (albeit mistakenly) for belief *q* for me but not for you.

A defeater for a particular belief *q*, then, is simply another belief *p*, given my noetic structure at a particular point in time, such that I cannot hold to *q* given that I believe *p*.[2] In some cases, one has only a partial defeater—perhaps one may not have yet realized the connection between *p* and *q* such that *p* was a defeater for *q*. Consider the following case again. Frege once believed that:

> For every condition or property P, there exists the set of just those things that have P.[3] (Hereafter FS.)

Bertrand Russell, in a letter to Frege, pointed out that FS has serious problems. If FS is true, then there exists the "the set of non-self mem-

2. Ibid., 361.
3. Ibid.

bered sets because there is the property or condition of being non-self-membered."[4] However, if such a set did exist that would mean that it would exemplify itself only if it did not exemplify itself. This means it would exemplify and non-exemplify itself, which is a contradiction. So Frege did not have a defeater for FS until he read Russell's letter.

The specific type of defeater that I am concerned with is an epistemic defeater. An epistemic defeater may nullify the belief's positive epistemic status, or at the least will decrease the belief's positive epistemic status such that one may have reduced confidence in the belief or perhaps may give up the belief. An epistemic defeater may be a rational or warrant defeater, but my focus will primarily be on rational defeaters. This is because the Christian exclusivist that we are concerned with is someone who has reflected on the diversity of religious beliefs and their mutually exclusive nature, and still holds to her exclusivism. That is, she believes that she is rational in her belief that CE even in the face of competing mutual beliefs.

Plantinga defines an epistemic defeater as such:

> D is a purely epistemic defeater of B for S at t if and only if (1) S's noetic structure N at t includes B and S comes to believe D at t, and (2) any person S^* (a) whose cognitive faculties are functioning properly in the relevant respects, (b) who is such that the bit of the design plan governing the sustaining of B in her noetic structure is successfully aimed at truth (i.e., at the maximization of true belief and minimization of false belief) and nothing more, (c) whose noetic structure is N and includes B, and (d) who comes to believe D but nothing else independent of or stronger than D, would withhold B (or believe it less strongly).[5]

Pollock echoes similar sentiments:

> If P is a reason for S to believe Q, R is a defeater for this reason if and only if R is logically consistent with P and (P&R) is not a reason for S to believe Q.[6]

In each of the two cases the epistemic defeater forces the believer to give up a particular belief she used to hold.

---

4. Ibid.

5. Ibid., 363.

6. Pollock, *Contemporary Theories of Knowledge*, 38.

Given this brief discussion on defeaters, we can nuance my key question a bit further. There are many intelligent and sincere people in the world who hold to beliefs that are incompatible with CE. Does this fact serve as an epistemic defeater for the Christian exclusivist who holds to CE? More specifically, is a Christian exclusivist required to give up CE when faced with the facts of mutually exclusive religious beliefs? I will argue no.

THE SON OF GREAT PUMPKIN OBJECTION:
MARTIN AND DEROSE

Some have objected to Plantinga's Reformed Epistemological arguments based on a series of objections that Plantinga himself labels the Great Pumpkin Objection (hereafter GPO), and later on the Son of Great Pumpkin Objection (hereafter SGP). Although Plantinga himself raises the GPO objection, SGP is an objection that originates from Michael Martin.[7] Both objections basically claim that if belief in God is properly basic, then other beliefs can be properly basic—even beliefs which contradict the claims of Reformed Epistemologists like Plantinga. Keith DeRose claims that there are two objections that lurk within the realm of Plantinga's original GPO and Martin's SGP, and that Plantinga has only answered the easier objection and not the stronger one.[8] In this next section I will defend Plantinga from this charge.

Plantinga first introduces GPO by claiming this:

> If belief in God can be properly basic, why cannot *just any* belief be properly basic? Could we not say the same for any bizarre aberration we can think of? What about voodoo or astrology? What about the belief that the Great Pumpkin returns every Halloween? Could I properly take *that* as basic? Suppose I believe that if I flap my arms with sufficient vigor, I can take off and fly about the room; could I defend myself against the charge of irrationality by claiming this belief is basic? If we say that belief in God is properly basic, will we not be committed to holding that just anything, or nearly anything, can properly be taken as basic, thus throwing wide the gates to irrationalism and superstition?[9]

7. Martin, *Atheism.*

8. DeRose, "Voodoo Epistemology."

9. Plantinga, "Reason and Belief in God."

The main concern here is that belief in God, if it were to be accepted as properly basic, would open the door to irrationalism. This would include embracing strange beliefs such as voodoo, astrology, the belief that the Great Pumpkin returns every Halloween, and the belief that one can fly while flapping one's arms. Regardless of how one views these beliefs, in particular voodoo and astrology since they are taken quite seriously by fairly large communities of people, the important notion is that the objector is claiming that there are beliefs that Plantinga would not accept as properly basic. If not, why not, asks the objector? After all, these beliefs could seemingly be properly basic in the same way that the Reformed Epistemologist's belief in God is properly basic the objector claims.

DeRose claims there are two questions here, an easy question and a hard question. The easy question asks, "Is Plantinga committed to weird and bizarre beliefs leading to irrationality by claiming that belief in God is properly basic"? Plantinga answers no:

> So, the Reformed epistemologist can properly hold that belief in the Great Pumpkin is not properly basic, even though he holds that belief in God is properly basic and even if he has no full-fledged criterion of proper basicality. Of course he is committed to supposing that there is a relevant *difference* between belief in God and belief in the Great Pumpkin if he holds that the former but not the latter is properly basic. But that should prove no great embarrassment; there are plenty of candidates. These candidates are to be found in the neighborhood of the conditions that justify and ground belief in God—conditions I shall discuss in the next section. Thus, for example, the Reformed epistemologist may concur with Calvin in holding that God has implanted in us a natural tendency to see his hand in the world around us; the same cannot be said for the Great Pumpkin, there being no Great Pumpkin and no natural tendency to accept beliefs about the Great Pumpkin.[10]

The Reformed Epistemologist need not have any commitment to the belief that the Great Pumpkin returns every year on Halloween. Plantinga is not committed to the claim that the beliefs of the followers of the Great Pumpkin are properly basic since Plantinga clearly does not see the conditions that ground belief in God as being equal to that of the Great Pumpkin. Plantinga's claim here is that belief in the Great Pumpkin is unjustified. This is the answer to the easy question DeRose claims.

10. Ibid., 78.

The hard question falls out of SGP. Plantinga claims that this passage of Martin encapsulates the main thesis of the SGP objection:

> Although reformed epistemologists would not have to accept voodoo beliefs as rational, voodoo followers would be able to claim that insofar as they are basic in the voodoo community they are rational and, moreover, that reformed thought was irrational in this community. Indeed, Plantinga's proposal would generate many different communities that could *legitimately* claim that their basic beliefs are rational . . . Among the communities generated might be devil worshipers, flat earthers, and believers in fairies, just so long as belief in the devil, the flatness of the earth, and fairies was basic in the respective communities.[11]

The hard question acknowledges that neither Plantinga nor the Pumpkinites (or devil worshipers or believers in fairies) are committed to the other's beliefs as properly basic. However, the hard question asks whether the Pumpkinites can use Plantinga's defense as well as Plantinga can? Plantinga reformulates Martin's objection into an SGP argument:

1) If Reformed epistemologists can legitimately claim that belief in God is rationally acceptable in the basic way, then for any other belief accepted in some community, the epistemologists of that community could legitimately claim that *it* was properly basic, no matter how bizarre the belief.

2) The consequent of 1 is false.

3) Therefore, the Reformed epistemologist can't legitimately claim that belief in God is rationally acceptable in the basic way.[12]

Plantinga's response to this is that Martin has loosely stated the argument in that he hasn't given what he means by the terms "rational" and "legitimately." Consider Martin's use of voodoo beliefs. Martin's point hinges not on voodooism, which he uses as an example, but any belief community that endorses strange beliefs that we normally do not accept. For example, in certain sects of voodooism one can put a curse on someone by going to a soothsayer and spilling the blood of a chicken into a metal plate.[13] The one who is cursed then would have bad luck in their

11. Martin, *Atheism*, 272.

12. Plantinga, *Warranted Christian Belief*, 346.

13. This is an actual practice of voodooism done in Haiti. I was told this by a former Haitian practitioner of voodoo and observed similar practices during a visit to Haiti in 1994.

life until the curse was lifted. What Plantinga seems to have in mind are beliefs like the aforementioned beliefs, which he would deem irrational. There are three primary candidates for rationality Plantinga considers: rationality as justification, internal rationality, and rationality as warrant in his response to Martin.

First, Plantinga claims that rationality as justification is the weakest candidate. This is because the voodooist could be within his intellectual rights in thinking what he thinks, at least in terms of not shirking an epistemic duty, and be justified on this account internally. Plantinga says of this that:

> We needn't linger long over rationality as justification: obviously the voodooists could be within their intellectual rights in think-ing what they do think (if only by virtue of cognitive malfunc-tion); hence they could be justified . . .[14]

The epistemologists of the voodoo community could legitimately claim that their voodoo beliefs were justified, hence premise 2) of Martin's argument is false with respect to justification. Second, Plantinga claims that the voodooist could also be internally rational. A belief is internally rational according to Plantinga if it is both a) produced by "faculties functioning properly 'downstream from experience' given your experi-ence (including doxastic experience) at the time in question" and b) that experience is completely compatible with proper functionality in terms of accepting the particular belief. This could be so for the voodooists, Plantinga states, in much the same way it could be so for the Christian exclusivist. So the voodoo epistemologists could no doubt know that the voodooists are internally rational in making such judgments about their voodoo beliefs, and hence report this fact. So premise 2) of Martin's ar-gument above fails for internal rationality in the same way that it did for rationality as justification.

So that leaves the third and final candidate, rationality as warrant. If this is what Martin means by rational, we can view premise 1) of the argument as such:

> If Reformed epistemologists can legitimately claim that belief in God is warranted in the basic way, then for any other belief ac-cepted in some community, the epistemologists of that commu-nity could legitimately claim that *it* was properly basic, no matter how bizarre the belief.

14. Plantinga, *Warranted Christian Belief*, 346.

Plantinga claims that the problem with this, of viewing rationality as warrant here, is that the Reformed epistemologist (namely Plantinga) does not claim that belief in God *is* in fact warranted.[15] This is because Christian belief would likely have warrant only if true, and Plantinga claims that he is not arguing that Christian belief is in fact true even though he believes them to be true. Now suppose theistic belief is properly basic with respect to warrant. Plantinga claims of the voodoo beliefs that:

> It doesn't follow, of course, that the voodoo epistemologist is also warranted in claiming that voodoo belief is properly basic with respect to warrant. For suppose voodoo belief is in fact false, and suppose further that it arose originally in some kind of mistake or confusion, or out of a fearful reaction to natural phenomena of one sort or another . . . then those original voodoo beliefs do not possess warrant.[16]

So the mere fact that the voodooist is claiming warrant for his beliefs does not show that his beliefs have warrant. The Reformed Epistemologist's claim that "Christian belief is likely to be warranted if true," would be different from the voodooist's claim that "Voodoo beliefs are likely to be warranted if true" if in fact voodoo beliefs are false. So it could certainly happen that voodoo beliefs are false, and thus are not legitimate in the sense of being warranted. So on such a scenario the voodooist's beliefs are not on the same epistemic footing as the Christian exclusivist. This would be the case if in fact Christian belief were true, and voodoo beliefs were false. Hence, Plantinga claims that it is not the case that:

> . . . if the claim that belief in God and in the great things of the gospel is properly basic with respect to warrant is itself warranted, then by the same token the claim that voodoo belief is properly basic with respect to warrant is itself warranted. Martin's argument, construed as we are currently construing it, therefore fails, its first premise is false.[17]

Plantinga concludes that SGP does no better than GPO, since Martin's complaints are multiply ambiguous and show no promise at all. That is, the situation between Christian beliefs and voodoo beliefs are disanalogous.

15. Ibid., 347.
16. Ibid., 348.
17. Ibid., 349.

Of this particular response, DeRose claims that Plantinga's treatment of Martin's argument is unfair and that Plantinga has not answered the hard question that Martin points to. Rather, DeRose claims that Plantinga has only answered the easy question. DeRose formulates the hard question as such:

> The question is whether Plantinga's use of the strategy is any more successful, or cogent, perhaps, than is the Pumpkinite's. To the objector, it seems that, and there seems to be nothing to block the conclusion that, to use Plantinga's own phrase, Plantinga's defense is "no better than" the Pumpkinites' defense.[18]

To see clearly what exactly this objection entails, consider a few questions that Plantinga raises that are within the realm of the hard question. First, Plantinga asks:

> Now couldn't this be argued with equal cogency with respect to any set of beliefs, no matter how weird?[19]

The qualifying statement is "no matter how weird." Plantinga's strategy is to answer as follows:

> Certainly not. Many propositions are not such that if they are true, then very likely they have warrant: the proposition *No beliefs have warrant* comes to mind.[20]

The key here is in understanding Plantinga's view of warrant as it relates to his religious epistemology. He is arguing that Christian belief is likely to be warranted only *if* true. Plantinga is merely pointing out here that not just any set of beliefs will have this particular feature:

F   If P is true, then P is likely to be warranted.

It's clear that self-undermining beliefs can't be held in the basic way and the like. Plantinga has argued that Christian belief *does* have feature F.

Next, Plantinga raises another question that is within the realm of the hard question given his previous answer:

> But, you say, isn't this just a bit of logical legerdemain; are there any systems of belief seriously analogous to Christian belief for which these claims cannot be made?[21]

---

18. DeRose, "Voodoo Epistemology."
19. Plantinga, *Warranted Christian Belief*, 350.
20. Ibid.
21. Ibid.

So the question that comes from this is: couldn't someone argue for their own mutually exclusive religious belief systems in the same way as Plantinga has? If so, doesn't this mean that any set of beliefs that are seriously analogous to Christian belief can be argued for in the same way that Plantinga has argued for Christian belief? Plantinga's answer is that certain religions such as Judaism, Islam, and certain forms of Hinduism, Buddhism, and Native American religion could use his strategy to defend their beliefs.[22] However, Plantinga claims that his strategy would not work for just any sort of beliefs, since there are clear examples of beliefs that are irrational in nature.

This now leads DeRose to the pointed question which he puts in the form of an anti-Plantinga argument (hereafter, argument PQ):

1) There are some possible wildly bizarre/weird aberrations of irrationalism that are Plantinga-defensible (i.e., are such that Plantinga's defensive strategy against the charge of irrationality would be as successful in defense of them as it is in Plantinga's hands in defense of Christian belief).

2) Plantinga's strategy could not be used to successfully defend the wildly bizarre/weird aberrations against the charge of irrationality.

3) Therefore, Plantinga's defensive strategy does not provide a successful defense of Christian belief against the charge of irrationality.

DeRose points out that the key here is the claim that there are certain beliefs that are irrational but can be Plantinga-defensible. Why would Plantinga claim that on several senses of "rational" the voodooists or pumpkinites would be rational here, when earlier he seems to have claimed they are not? It matters not whether there are forms of voodoo that can be rational, since the hard question is concerned with irrational beliefs and not specifically with voodooism as a belief system. The SGP objector need not be committed to the view that all voodoo is irrational or even that voodoo is in fact irrational, just that there are irrational beliefs held by some that seem to be able to be Plantinga-defensible. (Suppose we consider the previously mentioned chicken blood curse belief as an irrational voodoo belief.) This is the harder question according to DeRose that Plantinga has not answered.

22. Ibid.

THE SON OF GREAT PUMPKIN OBJECTION: A RESPONSE

The answer to the hard or pointed question is this: there are several candidates for rationality and the voodooist *could* be rational on some of those accounts of rationality. So if we turn to argument PQ, the key is premise 1) there are some possible wildly bizarre/weird aberrations of irrationalism that are Plantinga-defensible (i.e., are such that Plantinga's defensive strategy against the charge of irrationality would be as successful in defense of them as it is in Plantinga's hands in defense of Christian belief). What exactly would it mean for Plantinga to affirm beliefs such as voodoo or belief in the Great Pumpkin as rational or irrational?

Consider again, F, the feature that Plantinga has argued for regarding warranted Christian belief. One answer for Plantinga in assessing certain beliefs such as voodoo or belief in the Great Pumpkin as rational or irrational may be to see if that belief has feature F. Perhaps the difference between these irrational beliefs and Christian belief could be that while the former *can* be shown to be true or false the latter, at least on Plantinga's view, cannot. Consider the belief that the Great Pumpkin returns every Halloween. This belief could easily be falsifiable. One could wait at the places where the Great Pumpkin is supposed to return, and confirm or disconfirm that the Great Pumpkin actually arrives. So perhaps all Plantinga has to do in answering the pointed question is to point to the fact that certain belief systems have feature F and certain belief systems do not. Those that do have feature F fall into two further categories: F_1 and F_2.

F_1 A belief system, as a whole, that can be reasonably verified as true or false to those who do not already accept the belief system.

F_2 A belief system, as a whole, that cannot be reasonably verified as true or false to those who do not already accept the belief system.

Clearly for Plantinga, Christian belief falls under F_2. So certain beliefs are sufficiently similar to Christian belief in that they may have feature F. (Though Plantinga believes Christian belief is warranted and true, he does not argue for the warrant and truth of Christian belief.) The belief that the Great Pumpkin returns every Halloween for example is a belief that may have feature F, and thus is analogous to Christian belief in one sense. However, belief in the Great Pumpkin falls under category F_1 and thus is not analogous to Christian belief. If so, the particular belief can be left by the wayside as *irrational* since the belief system can be shown to be false. Certain aspects of voodoo, the belief that I can fly if I flap my wings, and other aberrant beliefs may also fall under F_1 and thus are not analogous to Christian belief.

What happens if a belief system displays feature F but falls under F_2 and cannot be reasonably verified as true or false to those who do not already accept the belief system as true? In other words, what if a belief system is sufficiently analogous to Christian belief such that it cannot be verified as true or false to those who do not already the belief system as true? What if the epistemologists of the community of that particular belief system would endorse their belief system in much the same way Plantinga endorses Christian belief? This is not very problematic on Plantinga's view. Plantinga claims that certain religions such as Judaism, Islam, and certain forms of Hinduism, Buddhism, and American Indian religion could use his strategy to defend their beliefs. If these belief systems have feature F and fall under category F_2, and Plantinga seems to affirm they do, then they can be warranted in the same way that Christian belief can be warranted *if* the beliefs were true. That is, *if* the belief is true, then the belief is likely to be warranted. The fact that there are mutually exclusive belief systems that have feature F, none of which can be shown conclusively to be true or false to those who do not already accept the belief, does nothing to take away the fact that each belief system has feature F independent of one another.

Consider an example. Suppose every major religious belief system has feature F. Let us label these major religious belief systems A-n. If we substitute A-n for P in feature F, we get the following:

1. If religion A is true, then religion A is likely to be warranted.

2. If religion B is true, then religion B is likely to be warranted.

3. If religion C is true, then religion C is likely to be warranted.

. . . If religion n is true, then religion n is likely to be warranted.

Suppose further that each of these A-n religions falls under category F_2:

1. The major beliefs of religion A cannot be reasonably verified as true or false to those who do not already accept the belief as true. That is, no argument can be offered on behalf of the major beliefs of religion A so that those who were not already convinced of the truth of A would accept the argument.

2. The major beliefs of religion B cannot be reasonably verified as true or false to those who do not already accept the belief as true. That is, no argument can be offered on behalf of the major beliefs of religion B so that those who were not already convinced of the truth of B would accept the argument.

3. The major beliefs of religion C cannot be reasonably verified as true or false . . .

. . . The major beliefs of religion n cannot be reasonably verified as true or false . . .

Suppose further that one of the religious beliefs systems in A-n is actually true and thus likely to be warranted. Notice that this does nothing to take away each of the mutually exclusive religious belief systems A-n having feature F, since they fall under category F_2. That is, it could be the case that all the major mutually exclusive religious belief systems A-n have feature F and only one of them be true. Hence, multiple mutually exclusive belief systems may have feature F *and* fall under category F_2. Plantinga's strategy is to claim not only that Christian belief has feature F, but that it falls under F_2 and not F_1. If another belief system has feature F and falls under F_2, the belief system can be considered an analogue of Christian belief in the way Plantinga has outlined. If another belief system has feature F but falls under F_1, the belief system can be disregarded as irrational unless it is verified as true.[23]

As stated previously in this chapter, DeRose claims that Plantinga has misformulated Martin's objection in Plantinga's SGP argument by making it unnecessarily weak. DeRose offers what he claims was the stronger version (and true intention of Martin) in argument PQ. Consider argument PQ again. On the account I just sketched of F, F_1, and F_2, Plantinga would deny premise 1) of argument PQ since PQ fails

---

23. Plantinga lists a few examples including, 1) the belief that the earth is flat and 2) Humean skepticism.

to make the distinction between those belief systems that have feature F and fall under F_1 and those that have feature F and fall under F_2. That is, Plantinga can reject the claim that there are some possible wildly bizarre/weird aberrations of irrationalism that are Plantinga-defensible. Plantinga's defense strategy against the charge of irrationality for CE would *not* be as successful in defense of them as it is for Christian belief, since Christian belief has feature F and falls under F_2 and not F_1. On the account I have just sketched, mutually exclusive communities or weird aberrations of irrationalism that claimed their beliefs were basic in the same way as Plantinga does for Christian belief are not defensible in the same way as CE. Clearly the sense Plantinga aims for with his defense of CE or Christian belief is F_2 and not F_1.

What of the belief systems that have feature F and falls under F_2? The fact that there can exist mutually exclusive religious belief systems that have feature F and fall under F_2 is not a problem for the Reformed Epistemologist, since Plantinga does not claim that he can show that Christian belief is true even though he believes it is true. Again, on the account I have just sketched, the fact that other belief systems can claim feature F in an analogous way to Christian belief is not problematic since the goal of Plantinga's Reformed Epistemological defense is not to convince others of the truth of Christian belief. Rather the goal is to argue that "if Christian belief is true, then it likely has warrant" which of course is entirely different from arguing that "Christian belief is true" or even that "Christian belief has warrant." The fact that there are other religious belief systems that also have feature F does not derail the project of Reformed Epistemologists such as Plantinga since it is entirely possible for mutually exclusive belief systems with feature F to exist—even if only one of them were actually true.

So GPO does not serve as a defeater to the Reformed Epistemologist's defense of CE since the Reformed Epistemologist need not be committed to the claim that the beliefs of the followers of the Great Pumpkin are properly basic since the Reformed Epistemologist clearly does not see the conditions that justify and ground belief in God as equal to that of the Great Pumpkin. As for SGP, we see that the Reformed Epistemologist will clearly reject the first premise of Martin's objection:

> If Reformed epistemologists can legitimately claim that belief in God is rationally acceptable in the basic way, then for any other belief accepted in some community, the epistemologists of that

community could legitimately claim that *it* was properly basic, no matter how bizarre the belief.

On the account I have just sketched, the epistemologists of an irrational belief community could *not* claim that just any beliefs were properly basic since some of them fall under F_1 and can reasonably be shown as false. We also saw earlier that argument PQ, which is the stronger version of SGP, fails as an objection since the Reformed Epistemologist can reject premise 1 in PQ given the difference between analogues of Christian belief that have a) feature F and fall under F_1 and b) those that have feature F and fall under F_2. Thus GPO, SGP, and argument PQ (the stronger version of SGP) do not amount to a significant objection against the Reformed Epistemologist's defensive strategy against the charge of irrationality and thus do not serve as defeaters to Christian belief.

5

The Internalist Criterion
and the Inadequacy Thesis

IN THIS CHAPTER I examine two prominent objections to Plantinga's Reformed Epistemological defense of CE that argue that his defense is inadequate.

REFORMED EPISTEMOLOGY
AND THE INTERNALIST CRITERION: WILLARD

Julian Willard characterizes Plantinga's Reformed Epistemological attempts at resolving the problem of religious diversity as inadequate in defending Christian belief. Willard's primary thesis is that Plantinga has neglected the actual (both intellectual and doctrinal) commitments of religious believers as well as fail to account for the "intellectual obligation" that is at work in such cases of conflicting religious belief with respect to pluralism.[1] He concludes that without an internalist defense of CE, versus the Reformed Epistemologist's externalist defense of CE, mutually exclusive religious beliefs with respect to CE do serve as defeaters for CE.[2]

---

1. Willard, "Plantinga's Epistemology." Please note the specific nuances between PRD, which is an argument with specific premises and conclusion, and the problem of religious diversity (written in lower case letters) which simply claims that one cannot hold to any form of religious exclusivism due to the sheer amount and diversity of religious practitioners in the world.

2. As was seen earlier in chapter 2, epistemic internalist accounts of justification or warrant are accounts that claim that *all* of the factors needed for a belief to be epistemically justified or warranted for a given person be cognitively accessible to that person, internal to his cognitive perspective. The externalist thesis is simply a denial of the internalist account. Hence, the externalist can claim that *some* of the factors needed for a belief to be epistemically justified or warranted for a given person be cognitively ac-

Willard primarily attributes to Plantinga the view that the particular epistemic status given to a person's religious belief is secondary in nature when compared to one's metaphysical or theological beliefs. The claim is that one's metaphysical commitments precede one's epistemic commitments. For example, one wouldn't commit epistemically to Christian belief or CE unless one already had a metaphysical commitment to a Christian worldview. The Christian exclusivism defended by Plantinga concludes that certain religious beliefs can be prima facie warranted, even though there may be no positive argument that can be given for Christian belief. The belief that God exists or beliefs such as "God is speaking to me" or "God disapproves of what I've done" are beliefs that can be accepted by the Christian exclusivist without appeal to any positive argument on Plantinga's religious epistemology. Perhaps the metaphysical commitment that God exists came about via a religious experience of sorts, or through reading a particular religious text, etc. So the metaphysical status of Christianity may be true, false, actual, possible, or whatever else. However, Willard claims that discussion of the epistemic status of Christian belief is to discuss the warrant, rationality, or justification of beliefs held by persons—either actual or possible. Since one of Plantinga's main goals is to provide a way for the Christian community to think about the epistemic status of their beliefs, for Plantinga's project to succeed the hypothetical person holding to Christian belief in his model must have beliefs that are analogous to actual beliefs held by Christians.[3] So the key claim by Willard is that one cannot separate the actual beliefs held by Christians from the beliefs generated by Plantinga's extended A/C model in assessing Plantinga's project epistemically.

The operative question for Willard, as we shall see, is this: *do* religious believers give up (or perhaps modify) their religious belief in the face of awareness of religious diversity? Willard will argue that the answer to this question is crucial in assessing Plantinga's Reformed Epistemological defense of CE since, according to Willard, a believer should not lose confidence in her beliefs simply due to the existence of rival religious beliefs. Willard's goal is not merely an empirical claim

cessible to that person without claiming that *all* of the factors be cognitively accessible since externalism is simply a denial of the internalist thesis. Though Willard does not use the word 'defeater' in his essay, he clearly argues that Plantinga's externalist views are untenable with regard to his exclusivism and the problem of religious diversity.

3. Beilby makes this particular point in *Epistemology as Theology*. Beilby and Willard hold similar views on this aspect of Plantinga's project.

based on some study of religious believers (though he concedes that he is unable to confirm any empirical claim that most actual believers do respond a particular way), but rather to highlight how the answer to this question is a challenge to Plantinga's Reformed Epistemological response to the problem of religious diversity.

Any particular religious community is going to think that their own religious beliefs are more likely to be true than their rivals. So if a particular exclusivistic religious community is committed to the view that any non-believer has a noetic defect or cognitive corruption of sorts, that particular community cannot embrace other religious views in the same way as their own.[4] For example, in Christianity (broadly construed) there exists a tradition of natural theology. Natural theology typically consists of giving positive intellectual apologetic arguments in defense of the Christian faith. The implicit assumption in natural theology is that the non-Christian is on similar epistemic footing with the Christian with respect to their noetic faculties, at least those particular faculties that are required for evaluating natural theological arguments.

This is because there would be no reason, according to Willard, to advance an argument for the existence of God or any other Christian belief that would benefit the non-believer unless he were at least approximately on epistemic par with the believer such that the non-believer would appreciate the force of such an argument. So natural theology in the Christian tradition presupposes that the noetic faculties of the non-Christian are similar to the Christian such that the non-Christian *could* potentially be convinced by such arguments in favor of the Christian faith. The denouement of all this Willard claims is that "any religious community that embraces such an intellectual tradition cannot at the same time consistently endorse Plantinga's externalist approach."[5] This is primarily because a Reformed Epistemological externalist approach rejects natural theology as described by Willard above and regards the non-believer as not functioning properly with regards to the *sensus divinitatis*.

Willard claims there is a tension between Plantinga's externalism with regards to proper function and religious belief versus natural theology. Willard claims that Plantinga seems to affirm both of the following two propositions:

4. Willard, "Plantinga's Epistemology," 283.
5. Ibid.

1) Natural theology may serve to loosen the "corruption that sin has upon the intellectual faculties of the non-believer."[6]

2) Natural theology may *increase* the warrant for a believer, though natural theology is not needed for one to hold to Christian belief.[7]

Willard claims natural theology aligns with epistemic internalism, since the warrant for the conclusion of an argument for religious belief would be cognitively accessible to both the believer and non-believer. While 1) is not really problematic for Plantinga, Willard claims it does serve an important point. On Plantinga's account, natural theology may give someone additional confidence in terms of supposing her religious beliefs are more likely to be true than its rivals even if the arguments are not what actually convinces the non-believer to accept the religious belief.

Willard argues that 2) is problematic since Plantinga does not explain *why* it is the case that natural theology would increase the warrant for a believer. According to Willard, Plantinga's account is such that epistemic factors that are cognitively accessible to a person are neither necessary nor sufficient with regards to warrant for any religious belief. The problem is that Plantinga concludes that for some Christians, an awareness of religious pluralism would reduce the confidence of their Christian belief.[8] Given his epistemic externalism, Plantinga cannot explain *why* it is that a Christian exclusivist would lose confidence in their religious belief because on Plantinga's account of warrant:

> . . . for any proposition p, no matter what internally-available grounds or markers one has for one's belief that p, it is possible that in fact one's cognitive faculties are malfunctioning in forming the belief that p, and thus that one does not know that p, even if p is true. And conversely, even if one does in fact know that p, one may perfectly well have very poor grounds or markers for one's belief that p.[9]

So Willard is alluding to the inability of a believer to adjudicate between a) whether one's cognitive faculties are functioning properly, b) whether one in fact knows p, and c) whether p is true.

6. Ibid., 284.

7. Plantinga, "Two Dozen (or so) Theistic Arguments."

8. Plantinga, *Warranted Christian Belief*, 456.

9. Willard, "Plantinga's Epistemology," 286.

Willard concludes that there would be no decision procedure for any subject S then, on this sort of externalism, to determine their degree of confidence in knowing the particular religious belief. Plantinga's only answer to the doubting believer, someone who begins to suspect that her belief is an unconscious result of wish-fulfillment rather than as a result of the *sensus divinitatis*, is that the cognitive mechanism of the believer is aimed at truth and in an appropriate environment. In other words, Willard is claiming that Plantinga has not given much in terms of confidence for the believer in determining whether her cognitive faculties are in fact reliable.

The outcome of this is that Willard characterizes Plantinga's account as misrepresenting the actual epistemic (and theological) situation of a Christian believer with respect to their religious beliefs. Willard claims there may be an important internalist criterion in Plantinga's approach, one he labels C:

C   One who holds a given belief p, must be aware of no belief that conflicts with p, unless he has good reason for holding that p can be shown to be more likely to be true than its rival(s).[10]

So if a person believes in p, then he must not be aware of another belief (held by himself or by others) that conflicts with p without knowing of an argument for why p is to be preferred over its rival(s). So if person A holds belief p and person B holds belief ~p, according to C, person A would have to believe that p can be shown to be more likely to be true than ~p. That is, only one of the beliefs p or ~p can be true or correct at a particular time. Both p and ~p cannot be true at the same time, given that they are conflicting beliefs. A stipulation in C, adds Willard, is that two people with the exact same noetic structure may differ with respect to C since only one of them may be aware of a conflicting religious belief. Plantinga, of course, concedes that the Christian exclusivism he defends is one where the exclusivist is completely aware of the diversity of religious beliefs pursued by other people of great intelligence and sincerity.

Willard concedes that he employs a deontological epistemic concept, even though we rarely have direct voluntary control over our beliefs. So one may not be able to alter one's beliefs in the same way one could open a door or answer a question, but one can *indirectly* go about altering one's

10. Ibid., 287.

belief-forming and activities that were a part of the original belief. For example, one can indirectly influence one's dispositions even though one may not directly be able to do so. Willard understands this commitment as "S has a good reason for belief q just if S is not violating any relevant intellectual duties or obligations in forming and holding q in the way he does."[11] The requirement for C then is not that the believer in question must show that belief p is more likely to be true than q, but rather that he has good reason for believing that it "*can be shown* to be more likely to be true," which in this case means more likely to be true than its rivals.[12] So it may be that there are others he trusts, perhaps someone else in his belief community who can do this. Willard claims this is necessary to give credence to the social nature of human belief-forming cognitive practices. After all, we trust our parents, teachers, journalists, scientists, and other experts in this manner.

C for Willard is qualified, in the sense that he alleges that it is possible *in principle*—assuming that there are no contingent limitations on time, resources, and the like in the pursuing of C. Though this is quite difficult, to assess such a broad counterfactual with regard to C, Willard claims that careful considerations of analogical arguments (much like the ones employed by Plantinga) should make the accepting of C a plausible one. Willard claims that C strikes a balance between 1) "the overly harsh stipulation that one must have justified confidence that one's belief is, *here and now*, demonstrably epistemically superior to its rivals," and 2) "an overreliance on epistemological externalism in vindicating the intellectual credentials of one's belief."[13]

C demands, according to Willard, a response based on *internalist* epistemic rationality. So one's religious beliefs would be evaluated from the standpoint of maximizing truth and falsity without appeal to reliability or proper function since the subject in C has to be convinced that her religious beliefs are epistemically superior internally. That is, she would not be aware of any conflicting propositions that are more likely to be true. This aspect for C would rule out any response to the problem of religious diversity via any externalist notions such as the SD since one

---

11. Ibid. Willard in footnote 25 goes further to claim that this deontological thesis does not entail the controversial claim that forming and holding beliefs is (ever) under the direct control of the will; indirect control of the belief in question is sufficient.

12. Ibid., 288.

13. Ibid.

would need to be in cognitive possession of the warrant or justification that shows that p is preferable to its rival ~p. C is amply satisfied when we consider other more familiar practices such as sense perception, rational intuition, introspection and the like.

Willard claims that human beings are fundamentally committed to C in their common intellectual practices and that careful consideration of the analogies to the situation of religious diversity that Plantinga offers suggest that C may be true. Willard claims Plantinga makes this sort of claim: "the very fact that a particular belief, intuition, or evaluation is an element of our existing intellectual behavior is *itself* an important (though not decisive) source of positive epistemic status for that belief, intuition, or evaluation."[14] Willard claims that Plantinga could revoke this statement, but only at a cost that is central to Plantinga's work in religious epistemology. Willard's primary argument is of this form: (hereafter WP)

1) Human beings are committed to C—one who holds a given belief p, must be aware of no belief that conflicts with p, unless he has good reason for holding that p can be shown to be more likely to be true than its rival(s).

2) Plantinga's religious epistemology neglects C, which Plantinga himself concedes is an important part of coming to Christian belief.

3) Therefore, Plantinga's religious epistemology is deficient.

Willard is not making a normative claim or even claiming that this is *exactly* how people respond. Rather, his objection is rooted in something that he thinks is not only a consequence of Plantinga's externalism/Reformed Epistemology but also something Plantinga concedes himself.

Willard's objections to Plantinga have a root worry that Plantinga's religious epistemology is deficient in that it relies on epistemic externalism rather than internalism. If we consider WP, the key is premise 2) which claims that Plantinga's externalist religious epistemology neglects C which has an internalist component to it. This internalist component is primarily the view that one needs to be in cognitive possession of the justification or warrant for why it is that one would prefer belief

14. Ibid., 290.

p to its rival(s). This is not required on Plantinga's externalist proper-function account of warrant as was stated in chapter 2. The conclusion of Willard's primary argument is that Plantinga's Reformed Epistemological response to the problem of religious diversity is inadequate. If Willard were correct, the fact that there exist religious belief systems with mutually exclusive beliefs would serve as a defeater for CE given Plantinga's externalism. Willard is not committed to the view that there are no responses to the existence of rival religious beliefs being a defeater for CE, but claims that Plantinga's externalism/Reformed Epistemology does not provide a solution to the existence of rival religious beliefs being a defeater for CE.

Willard points out that Plantinga concedes that an awareness of religious diversity may reduce one's own confidence in one's Christian belief.[15] Given his externalism, why would Plantinga make such a claim? The core problem with such an account, according to Willard, is that the religious believer has no idea whether his cognitive faculties are functioning properly with regards to p. If the religious believer has no idea whether his cognitive faculties are functioning properly with regards to p, how could his confidence be reduced or increased by being aware of religious diversity? On Plantinga's account, regardless of the internally available grounds or markers for one's belief that p, it is still possible that one's cognitive faculties are malfunctioning. Why would the awareness of other religious beliefs that come into conflict with one's own religious beliefs reduce one's confidence? According to Willard, on Plantinga's account the religious believer lacks a decision procedure to determine a) the degree of confidence one should have with regard to the religious belief at hand, and b) the actual degree of confidence one has in the particular religious belief. This is problematic, according to Willard, since Plantinga argues that the Christian exclusivist can be confident in her beliefs.

REFORMED EPISTEMOLOGY
AND THE INTERNALIST CRITERION: A RESPONSE

Willard has missed the point of the purpose of natural theology on Plantinga's account of epistemic warrant and justification. Although natural theology typically does align with internalism as Willard points

---

15. Plantinga, *Warranted Christian Belief*, 456.

out, warrant on Plantinga's Reformed Epistemological account comes in *degrees*. Plantinga is not claiming that natural theology will *necessarily* loosen the "corruption that sin has" on a non-believer, rather that it *may* loosen it if the non-believer is able to acknowledge propositions such as CE. That is, natural theology may serve to trigger the SD in such a way that one is able to acknowledge propositions such as CE. Willard seems to be arguing that natural theology must lead to CE whereas Plantinga seems to be arguing that natural theology may play one part of a larger role. Along with the SD and other factors such as the instigation of the Holy Spirit, natural theology *may* loosen the "corruption that sin has" on a non-believer. Of course it need not go this way. One may simply come to belief in God through the SD. So her confidence that her cognitive faculties are in fact functioning properly may be boosted by such a belief in God and natural theology may play *one* rather than the whole part of such confidence, along with other factors including the triggering of the SD to form a belief about God. Natural theology, then, can play a dependent versus an independent role along with the SD in someone coming to Christian belief. On Plantinga's extended A/C model, natural theology does not play a role independent of the SD. Willard seems to argue that natural theology can play an independent role on Plantinga's Reformed Epistemological account, which seems to be mistaken.

Consider a non-believer who is exposed to some natural theology. Assume the non-believer one day comes to have a God-belief in much the same way one accepts a math axiom, they just seem to be true to her and she is unable to articulate why or why not in a way that satisfies those who do not already believe in God. Like a math axiom which one connects to one's other mathematical beliefs, she finds herself connecting her other beliefs to this God-belief. She sees that although she is functioning properly cognitively, she could not get over a seeming defeater for Christian belief—perhaps the problem of evil. Now, after being exposed to some natural theology she claims she has overcome her difficulty with the problem of evil. So though she considers herself warranted in her religious belief because of her basic belief in God, natural theology allowed her to overcome a philosophical defeater for her belief in God by *increasing* warrant for her Christian belief. So this is precisely why Plantinga claims that on his Reformed Epistemological account natural theology *may* increase the warrant of one's belief in God, even though one need not have such arguments to have a warranted belief in

God. Of course if warrant must be cognitively accessible to the knower, then Willard is correct in his objection that this would give the believer no confidence in her belief. However, on Plantinga's externalist proper-function account of warrant one need not be in cognitive possession of the warrant. The believer, if her beliefs are produced by a cognitive faculty functioning properly (subject to no cognitive malfunction) in a cognitive environment congenial for that faculty according to a design plan successfully aimed at truth, can have warrant for her beliefs even without the warrant being cognitively accessible to the believer/knower in this case.

So natural theology may play an internalist role (as Willard claims), if internalism is true. Or it may play an externalist role, in that the believer/knower need not be in cognitive possession of the warrant, if externalism is true. That is she need not produce an argument that shows her cognitive faculties are functioning properly to have confidence they are functioning properly. As I have outlined with how natural theology may serve a dependent role to the workings of the SD, this believer is already convinced via the SD that her beliefs are warranted. The believer is not in the same epistemic situation as the non-believer since she already accepts that the SD is reliable. On Plantinga's Reformed Epistemological account, SD beliefs about God and beliefs about the reliability of SD come about in the basic way without appeal to any independent argument. Willard's objection misses the mark in asking for an internalist reason. That is, he wants an independent argument that shows the SD is reliable to someone who is unconvinced by its reliability. Of course Plantinga and other externalists claim that none can be given. Unless Willard offers a non-question begging argument for the truth of internalism, his objection is deficient. As we have seen with Bonjour in chapter 2, it is unlikely that Willard can produce such an argument.

Next, Willard claims that the religious believer would have no confidence in her Christian belief given Plantinga's Reformed Epistemological externalist account. This objection presupposes that the only reasons available are internalist ones. Consider someone who is unable to see that the natural numbers have no end, (e.g. 1, 2, 3, . . . n) and go on infinitely. Suppose further that this person just does not see they go on infinitely even though there are people around him who try to explain that they do. Now, what exactly would be the argument one could give to such a person so that they have confidence that natural numbers have no end? It is clearly not a case of deductive reasoning. That is, no argument could be given to such a person where this person would accept the premises of the argument as true. If someone is asked by such a person who is unable to see that natural numbers have no end: *how do you know your cognitive faculties are functioning properly with respect to the belief that natural numbers have no end?* What sort of answer could be given that would convince this person? None can be given. Yet we hold such a belief as warranted even if we cannot give an answer that would satisfy this natural-number-skeptic. Plantinga could respond in much the same way to Willard when he questions how it is that someone can know if their cognitive faculties are functioning properly with respect to one's confidence in CE.

Willard claims that there would be no decision procedure on this sort of externalism for someone to determine one's degree of confidence in the particular religious belief. Put another way, Willard claims Plantinga has not given much in terms of confidence for the believer herself in determining whether her own cognitive faculties are in fact reliable. Of course this problem could be remedied if the internalist demand for an argument is satisfied, an argument that would show *why* the SD is reliable or *why* Christian belief is true. Plantinga claims that he is unable to give such an argument. The Reformed Epistemologist could reply in much the same way as the previous natural-numbers-being-infinite belief. Plantinga in his Reformed Epistemological defense is not arguing that Christian belief is true or even that it is in warranted, rather he argues that 'if Christian belief is true, then it probably does have warrant.' This does not mean he has no reasons for thinking that Christian belief is true or that SD beliefs are reliable, rather these beliefs are taken in the basic way.

Next, we turn to WP, Willard's primary anti-Plantinga argument. As we have seen previously, Willard's support for premise 1) that human beings are committed C is that Plantinga himself concedes that the actual belief practices of Christians is an important part of coming to Christian belief.[16] Support for premise 2) is that Plantinga's externalist warrant-as-proper-function account neglects C. That is, on Plantinga's account, someone can hold a belief p without having a good reason that p can be shown to be more likely to be true than its rivals. The challenge

16. Willard, "Plantinga's Epistemology," 290.

basically amounts to the idea that having a basic belief in CE or a basic belief in the reliability of the SD is inadequate.

Consider C again: one who holds a given belief p, must be aware of no belief that conflicts with p, unless he has good reason for holding that p can be shown to be more likely to be true than its rival(s). The key contention is what counts as a reason. Clearly, for Willard any appeal to reason is construed on an internality framework. That is, the reason must be such that it has cogency and could potentially convince those who disagreed that p can be shown more likely to be true than its rival(s). Could one *always* give such a reason that would satisfy those who disagreed in this particular situation?

Consider an example. Suppose you meet someone who is a skeptic about other minds. You of course demur and claim that other minds do exist, including your mind and that of the skeptic. He claims that he's unsure. You try to argue him out of his position but he is unconvinced. Consider condition C in this case. You hold a belief p and are aware of a belief p that conflicts with p, but you cannot give a reason that would satisfy those who disagree. Now, do you hold to C in this situation? That is, can you hold to your belief that other minds exist even though this belief cannot be shown to be more likely to be true than its rivals in an argument that would be accepted by those who disagree? On Plantinga's externalist account, the answer is yes. You do have a reason: you have a basic belief that other minds exist. Of course not just any belief can be properly basic, for example the belief that I can fly if I flap my arms as hard as I can cannot be properly basic. Still, this does not show that there are no beliefs that satisfy this criterion.

If there are beliefs that are properly basic and belief in God is basic, why is it a problem to point to this as an *externalist* reason for holding to such a belief? The externalist position is not that one *never* gives reasons for holding to a belief to be warranted, but that one *need not always* give reasons or one *need not always* give reasons that would satisfy everyone for one to be warranted in holding the belief that p. So even if one believes that one can *never* show to the satisfaction of everyone who disagrees that one's belief p is superior to one's rivals, as shown in the skepticism about other minds example earlier, it is enough on a proper function account for one to hold to one's CE beliefs as basic. It seems right to you and you are violating no epistemic duties in holding CE since you are cognitively functioning properly in holding the belief. If someone were to produce a convincing argument that showed that p is false or that ~p is preferable you would change your mind. Of course, Reformed Epistemologists such as Plantinga believe no such argument has been given. Plantinga offers his extended A/C model as a way to show that unless someone can show that Christian belief is false, then one cannot claim that Christian belief is unwarranted.

Plantinga, of course, believes that Christian belief is true:

> But *is* this true? This is the really important question. And here we pass beyond the competence of philosophy, whose main competence, in this area, is to clear away certain objections, impedances, and obstacles to Christian belief. Speaking for myself and of course not in the name of philosophy, I can say only that it does, indeed, seem to me to be true, and to be the maximally important truth.[17]

As is the case with the belief that there exist other minds, Plantinga is convinced that one cannot show that Christian belief is true. So unless someone offers a non-question begging argument that concludes that CE is false, Plantinga's Reformed Epistemological and external arguments do not neglect C. That is, a properly functioning person can hold to CE and claim that she does have a good reason for holding CE as true. What is the reason? Her basic belief in God and the SD. An externalist may agree with C but preface it such that one may have good *externalist-proper-function* reasons rather than *internalist* reasons for holding that p can be shown to be more likely to be true than its rival(s).

A properly functioning cognitive faculty can hold to a belief p, even if there are other beliefs that conflict with p and even if one cannot convince those who disagree that p is more likely to be true than its rivals. Willard, mistakenly, assumes that only internalist reasons are legitimate without an argument for such. WP then does not serve as a defeater to Plantinga's Reformed Epistemological defense of CE.

THE INADEQUACY THESIS: BAKER

Deane-Peter Baker argues that the extended A/C model is inadequate in showing that PC (if Christian belief is true, then it likely has warrant) is true since Plantinga has not given an argument that shows that

---

17. Plantinga, *Warranted Christian Belief*, 499.

Christian belief in fact *is* warranted to the non-believer.[18] This objection Baker labels the Inadequacy Thesis (hereafter IT).

Imagine someone who rejects CE, a non-believer, contesting the claim that belief in God is properly basic. On Plantinga's account, the non-believer has no reason to think that belief in God is properly basic since the non-believer's SD would be damaged or simply not working. That is, even if Plantinga has met his goal of defending PC, the non-believer has no real reason to think that Christian belief is in fact warranted and that should be the real crux of the issue according to Baker. He says of this that:

> ... the claim that the Reformed epistemologist's contention that belief in God is properly basic and therefore warranted, even if technically successful, offers nothing to make the unbeliever think that the believer is at least *likely* to be *in fact* warranted.[19]

Richard Swinburne echoes Baker's thoughts:

> There is, however, a monumental issue which Plantinga does not discuss, and which a lot of people will consider needs discussing. This is whether Christian beliefs *do* have warrant (in Plantinga's sense). He has shown that they do, if they are true; so we might hope for discussion of whether they are true.[20]

Evan Fales also echoes similar thoughts:

> Perhaps God has implanted within me a *sensus divinitatis* by the light of which I could come to know Him.... But how can I know whether this is so? How can Plantinga know it? Is Plantinga's "model" of our cognitive constitution correct, or merely a just-so story?[21]

This claim by Fales, like the ones echoed by Baker and Swinburne before it, does not challenge Plantinga's claim that Christian belief *can* be warranted if true. Rather, the challenge to Plantinga is to offer some further reason or argument that could convince the non-believer that the claims of the extended A/C model are *in fact* warranted. The objection is asking for something beyond what Plantinga offers in his Reformed

18. Baker, "Plantinga's Reformed Epistemology."
19. Ibid., 94.
20. Swinburne, "Plantinga on Warrant."
21. Fales, "Critical notice of Warranted Christian Belief."

Epistemological defense of CE. IT asks if Christian beliefs are true as Plantinga believes they are, even though Plantinga claims that he cannot show CE as true, how would a non-believer know that they are in fact warranted? According to IT, they could not.

If we put IT in the form of an argument, it has this general form:

1. Plantinga has not given any arguments to show that Christian belief is warranted.

2. Even if Plantinga has successfully argued for PC, this still does not give the non-believer any reason to accept that Christian belief is warranted.

3. Therefore, Plantinga's account is inadequate.

The argument for IT is not claiming that Plantinga has failed in arguing for his central claim PC. Rather, the claim is that Plantinga has offered only a negative apologetic in defending the internal consistency of Christian belief when what is required for the non-believer is a positive apologetic to convince her that Christian beliefs are in fact warranted. It's interesting to note that IT is a critique that comes from those who either hold to Christian belief as true or are very sympathetic to Christian belief. The key difference between these internal Christian critics (Baker, Swinburne, and Fales) and a Reformed Epistemologist like Plantinga is that the former all believe that natural theological arguments are epistemically necessary in showing the non-believer that Christian belief is likely warranted. Though Plantinga claims that natural theology can be useful and can "bolster and confirm; perhaps even to convince" the non-believer, they are not epistemically necessary.[22] Baker contends that Reformed Epistemologists such as Plantinga should take IT seriously, especially since Plantinga has written a book that he thinks should be taken seriously by those who do not hold to Christian belief and also by those who do hold to Christian belief but are epistemic internalists.

THE INADEQUACY THESIS: A RESPONSE

Baker contends that Plantinga must provide a response for *why* Christian belief is in warranted. That is, Baker wants some sort of natural theological argument; something that would convince the non-believer that Christian belief is in fact true or warranted. It's not clear why Plantinga

22. Plantinga, "Two Dozen (or so) Theistic Arguments."

needs to offer a factual response for the veracity of Christian belief, when he does not believe such a response is possible—at least not in a way that would be non-controversial to those who do not already accept CE.[23] Of course this doesn't mean that Christian belief is not factual nor does it mean that one has to offer a factual account in claiming that Christian belief *can* be warranted if Christian belief is true.

Plantinga's key contention is that the *de jure* objection to Christian belief cannot be separated from the *de facto* objection. That is, if Plantinga's Reformed Epistemological arguments are on target, one cannot claim that Christian belief is both unjustified or unwarranted (*de jure*) while at the same time claiming that she does not know or cannot know whether Christian belief is true (*de facto*). The reason for why Plantinga argues this way is twofold: a) to show that someone cannot argue that Christian belief is unjustified without also showing that it's false, and b) because Plantinga is convinced that there is no way to argue for the truth or falsity of Christian belief in such a way that someone who did not already agree with the conclusion would accept the premises of the argument. The goal of Plantinga's Reformed Epistemological defense of CE is to point out that the warrant of Christian belief is tied to the truth of the belief. Given this, there is no way (on his account) to argue for the truth or falsity of Christian belief in a non-controversial way.

IT objects that PC as a conditional conclusion gives nothing to convince the non-believer that the believer is at least *likely* to be in fact warranted. Clearly, on Plantinga's account, no non-believer would accept PC as satisfying in accepting Christian belief as true or in fact warranted since the goal of offering PC was something entirely different. This is precisely why Plantinga does not argue for the truth of Christian belief nor does he argue that Christian belief has warrant, even though he believes that Christian belief is true. Perhaps one can claim that PC was the *strongest* possible conclusion on Plantinga's Reformed Epistemological account. IT is not really an objection. IT asks for something, Plantinga argues, that cannot be given.

---

23. See Plantinga, *God and Other Minds*. Plantinga argues in *God and Other Minds* that there is no way to argue for the truth that other minds exist in such a way that the skeptic would be convinced, yet we hold that there are other minds and we find ourselves warranted in the claim that there are other minds. He argues the same is true of God, that there is no way to argue for or against the existence of God.

Baker agrees with Basinger who formulates what he labels Plantinga's Negative Apologetic Thesis (hereafter NAT):

> For a theist to be in a position to maintain justifiably that the basic religious beliefs formed by her religious faculties are properly basic—i.e., to be in a position to maintain justifiably that her basic formed beliefs are true even though she has no "positive epistemic reason" to think they are true—she is only obligated to defend herself against the claim that her religious faculties are not functioning properly—i.e., are not functioning as they are indeed to function or are not producing true beliefs.[24]

Baker claims that NAT is deficient if one has a goal of discovering truth. That is, one needs to offer a positive apologetic rather than NAT as Basinger claims for Plantinga.

As we have seen earlier, Baker contends that Reformed Epistemologists such as Plantinga should take IT seriously since Plantinga has given arguments that he thinks should be taken seriously by both those who do not hold to Christian belief and those who do hold to Christian belief but are epistemic internalists. However, this criticism misses the mark. Plantinga's aim was not to show that Christian belief *does* have warrant but that it is likely warranted if in fact Christian belief is true. There are many levels to taking an argument seriously, and Baker is asking Plantinga to offer something to those who are non-externalists so that they may take his externalist Reformed Epistemological arguments seriously. But, why should any Reformed Epistemologist do such a thing?

Given his goal of arguing for conditional conclusion PC, Plantinga has given arguments that can be taken seriously by those who do not hold to Christian belief. If someone wants to derail Plantinga's Reformed Epistemological defense of CE, one can try and argue that Christian belief lacks feature F or argue that Christian belief is false. Plantinga in offering a defense of CE does not claim philosophical immunity, since *anyone* can try to derail his project by arguing in such a manner. Not offering a factual response to the truth or warrant of Christian belief does not show that Plantinga is not taking the non-believer or the epistemic internalist seriously.

Is Plantinga's answer complete? Is it enough to simply argue for PC, a conditional conclusion, rather than offer something more for

24. Baker, "Plantinga's Reformed Epistemology," 100.

the non-believer or the epistemic internalist? The answer to this question depends on one's goals. Baker seems to have different goals than Plantinga. Baker, Swinburne, and Fales are all very sympathetic to CE and to Christian exclusivism. However, they all want more than PC offers—something that would convince the non-believer that Christian belief is warranted. They are invoking the "ought implies can" maxim. One of the reasons they believe Plantinga ought to provide an account that shows that Christian belief is *in fact* warranted, is that they believe it can be done.[25] Of course this is at odds with Plantinga's Reformed Epistemology since he is convinced that there is no argument that would persuade most of these other intelligent adherents of other religions and the anti-religious to Plantinga's own Christian exclusivist position. IT amounts to an objection that Plantinga's defense of CE is incomplete in that it doesn't offer the non-believer anything positive to change her position about the epistemic status of Christian belief. IT asks for something that Plantinga claims he cannot give. Of course, this does nothing to derail Plantinga's project. IT is neither a defeater nor an objection to the conclusion of my main argument that if Plantinga's proper function account is a reasonable account of warrant, then Plantinga's Reformed Epistemological defense of CE is reasonable.

25. See Swinburne, *Existence of God*. Swinburne argues that the existence of God is more probable than not.

6

The Central Issue of Religious Exclusivism

HICK ON THE CENTRAL ISSUE OF RELIGIOUS EXCLUSIVISM

IN THIS SECTION I will discuss two objections that John Hick offers in critiquing Plantinga's Reformed Epistemological defense of CE. Hick first claims that Plantinga has not addressed the central issue between religious exclusivism and religious pluralism.[1] The central issue according to Hick is:

> . . . how to make sense of the fact that there are other great world religions, belief in whose tenets is as epistemologically well based as belief in the Christian doctrinal system, and whose moral and spiritual fruits in human lives seem to be as valuable as those of Christian faith.[2]

Plantinga's main response is that the Christian does not think that the beliefs of these other religions is as "epistemologically well based" as her Christian beliefs.

Plantinga claims that Hick is unclear:

1) Is Hick claiming that the fact is there *isn't* any relevant epistemic difference between the Christian and these other beliefs (whether the exclusivist knows this or not) and *therefore* the exclusivist's stance is arbitrary?

2) Or, is he claiming that the exclusivist *himself* agrees that there is no relevant epistemic difference between his views and those

---

1. Hick, "Epistemological Challenge of Religious Pluralism," 280.
2. Plantinga, "Ad Hick," 295.

of the dissenters, but accepts his own anyway, thus falling into arbitrariness?[3]

If 1), Plantinga claims that Hick needs to produce an argument for the claim that the exclusivist's beliefs are not epistemically superior to other views that are mutually exclusive with her own. Plantinga claims that he has argued at length, as I have detailed in chapter 2, that the Christian is likely to think he is epistemically privileged in holding to his beliefs even when he cannot produce an argument that would convince those who disagree. Furthermore if PC is true, then Hick will have to produce a good argument whose conclusion is "it is very unlikely that Christian belief is true" to show that the Christian exclusivist's stance is arbitrary.[4] Plantinga claims that he doesn't see how Hick "could offer such an argument, and I'll bet he doesn't either."[5] This of course is to claim that in such a case, one could not offer an argument whose premises would be accepted by those who were not already convinced of the conclusion.

If 2), then the exclusivist would be arbitrary since the exclusivist concedes that the views of the dissenters are equivalent in strength to her own. Of course Plantinga claims the exclusivist does not, even when he cannot offer an argument that shows his position is in fact epistemically superior, claim that her position is equivalent epistemically with those who disagree with her. Consider again, the person who does not think that the natural numbers are infinite (e.g., 1, 2, 3, . . . n). Suppose this person just does not see they go on infinitely even though there are people around him who try to explain that they do. In this scenario, no argument can be given to show such a person that the natural numbers are actually infinite. If someone who does believe that the natural numbers are infinite is asked by such a person: *how do you know your cognitive faculties are functioning properly with respect to the belief that natural numbers have no end?* What answer can be given? None can be given. Likewise, one can hold to their Christian exclusivism on Plantinga's Reformed Epistemological account because that is precisely the response of a properly functioning cognitive faculty. Now considering such a person who does not believe that the natural numbers are infinite, Plantinga

---

3. Ibid.
4. Ibid.
5. Ibid.

concedes that no epistemic duties are violated.[6] However, this alone does not show that the views of such a person are equivalent in strength to those who claim that natural numbers are infinite. Plantinga claims something similar for CE. The existence of contradicting positions by itself does not show that these opposing views are equivalent in strength to CE. The exclusivist of course can be mistaken in her beliefs just like anyone else, but this too by itself does not show that she is being arbitrary in holding to her religious exclusivism. As is the case with the person who is convinced that natural numbers are infinite even when he cannot produce an argument for his conclusion, the Christian exclusivist is not being arbitrary in believing as she does even when she cannot produce an argument for her conclusion. She also would not concede that her views are epistemically equivalent in strength to those that disagree even when she cannot produce an argument for her conclusion that CE.

Although Plantinga does not mention this, Hick seems to be assuming the equal weight theory (EW) in claiming that the tenets of certain religions are epistemically equivalent. I have argued at length against EW and PRD in chapter 3. I argued that one need not give equal weight to all religious propositions, including those that are mutually exclusive to one's own religious propositions simply because they are held by someone who is an epistemic peer. That is, the mere presence of someone who holds to a proposition that contradicts a proposition I hold is not a good reason for me to give up my belief. Of course the other way for Hick to show that the tenets of certain religions are equally well-based epistemically is to give some sort of argument, an argument that is not based on EW, that shows that the religious propositions of all the great religions of the world are equal with respect to epistemic strength. Until he or anyone else does produce such an argument, the Christian-exclusivist who holds to her Christian belief is not being arbitrary in thinking her position is epistemically superior even when she cannot give an argument that would be accepted by those who disagree with her.

The second objection by Hick is aimed at the following claim by Plantinga:

> For suppose we concede that if I had been born in Madagascar rather than Michigan, my beliefs would have been quite different. . . . of course, the same goes for the pluralist. Pluralism isn't and hasn't been widely popular in the world at large; if the pluralist

6. Ibid., 297.

had been born in Madagascar, or medieval France, he probably wouldn't have been a pluralist. Does it follow that he shouldn't be a pluralist or that his pluralistic beliefs are produced in him by an unreliable belief producing process? I doubt it.[7]

Plantinga claims further that:

> No matter what philosophical and religious beliefs we hold and withhold (so it seems), there are places and times such that if we had been born there and then, then we would not have displayed the pattern of holding and withholding of religious and philosophical beliefs we *do* display.[8]

Plantinga is pointing out that our beliefs, religious or otherwise, would be different if we were born elsewhere or if we had a different upbringing. However, this fact alone doesn't determine whether the beliefs we hold in fact are rational or warranted. This could be so for both the exclusivist and the pluralist.

Hick objects and claims that:

> The conclusion that I have myself drawn from this is that a "hermeneutic of suspicion" is appropriate in relation to beliefs that have been instilled into one by the surrounding religious culture.[9]

Hick continues further that:

> The relativity of religious belief in the circumstances of birth does not, of course, show that claims to a monopoly of religious truth are unjustified; but it does I think warn us to look critically at such claims. . . . One is not usually a religious pluralist as a result of having been raised from childhood to be one, as (in most cases) one is raised from childhood to be a Christian or a Muslim or a Hindu, etc. Surely the cases are so different that the analogy fails.[10]

Hick's claim is that the circumstance of birth is not necessarily an indication that a religious belief is false, but that it should give one pause in holding such a belief. While someone raised a Christian, or a Muslim, or a Hindu was raised in a particular religious tradition the religious plural-

7. Plantinga, "Defense of Religious Exclusivism," 212.

8. Ibid.

9. Hick, "Epistemological Challenge of Religious Pluralism," 281.

10. Ibid.

ist typically is not raised in such an environment. Presumably, he comes to his religious pluralism via different means than a religious exclusivist who was raised as a religious exclusivist comes to his own beliefs.

Consider an example. Suppose both Hick and Plantinga were brought up to believe that racial intolerance is morally wrong. If both Hick and Plantinga were born elsewhere and brought up differently, then it's fairly likely that both of them might think differently about racial intolerance. Of course this doesn't show that either of them should change their views about the immorality of racial intolerance simply because their views might have been different had they been born and raised elsewhere. Plantinga then asks why should it be different for Christian belief? The Christian exclusivist can also concede that her Christian beliefs might have been different if she was born and raised elsewhere, but this fact alone doesn't show that she should change her views. Consider another example. Suppose there was an undiscovered island whose inhabitants believed the earth was flat. Does the fact that one's views on the flatness of the earth could have been different if one were born on such an island show that one should not hold to one's own beliefs simply because there exist others on such an island who were taught that the earth is flat?[11] Of course not.

Suppose even with all this that Hick is correct and we should apply a hermeneutic of suspicion in relation to beliefs that have been instilled into one by the surrounding religious culture. Consider statement S:

S   One should apply a hermeneutic of suspicion in relation to any belief that has been instilled into one by the surrounding religious culture.

What should fall under belief here? There seems to be no good reason to distinguish religious beliefs from other beliefs, including philosophical beliefs, since a religious belief is simply a subset of any other beliefs a person holds as true. These beliefs would include one's moral beliefs, political beliefs, etc. It's plausible to claim that our beliefs, religious or

11. Very few people who believe that the earth is round (vs. the earth being flat) have actually done any research to confirm this. They simply hold this belief based on what others they trust have told them. This is true of many beliefs, including the belief that people have walked on the moon, or that there are galaxies larger than our own, or that stars go supernova, etc. The simple fact that I have been taught to believe something by someone else and or have been influenced by my upbringing does not show that my belief is mistaken or false.

philosophical, would be different if we were born and raised elsewhere. Hick is claiming we should be suspicious of any belief that was instilled into one by the surrounding religious culture. Of course one can argue that Hick's belief that S was also instilled into Hick by his surrounding religious culture. Suppose we apply S unto the belief that S:

S_2 One should apply a hermeneutic of suspicion in relation to S, since S has been instilled into one by the surrounding religious culture.

Of course now, we have another problem. Should we accept S_2 or be suspicious of S_2? After all, S_2 was the byproduct of a particular environment and culture and was instilled by that particular surrounding environment and culture. So now we apply S unto the belief that S_2:

S_3 One should apply a hermeneutic of suspicion in relation to S_2, since S_2 has been instilled into one by the surrounding religious culture.

And of course we can do this for S_4, S_5, S_6, and so on ad infinitum. Hick would demur here of course. How is this case any different from what Hick has claimed? He may claim that only beliefs that were instilled from childhood count as such a belief, including beliefs that were instilled into one by being raised as a Christian or Muslim or Hindu. Or he may claim that one should be suspicious only of religious beliefs. Of course he thinks that religious pluralism is not such a belief. Why not? Unless Hick can give a clear argument as to why beliefs that were acquired later do not fall under his hermeneutic of suspicion, since it seems clear they were instilled into one by the surrounding culture, S isn't very coherent.

Perhaps I have been unfair. Perhaps Hick is not objecting that one should reject these beliefs that were instilled into one by the surrounding religious culture, but rather that one should simply be suspicious of such beliefs. Since he does concede that the circumstances of birth and culture do not show that "claims to a monopoly of religious truth are unjustified," perhaps all he means is that one should be wary of such beliefs and think critically through them. Of course if this is the case then it's really not much of an objection. Does S count as the sort of belief one should be suspicious about since it might have been one that was instilled in one from one's environment or culture? Unless Hick can offer a clear as argument as to why not, S seems to fall prey to the same hermeneutic of suspicion that Hick claims for the religious exclusivist. S as a statement seems not unlike the verification principle or Clifford's principle, in that it endorses a principle that it itself cannot sustain.[12]

Finally, it is unclear why the case for religious pluralism is really different from someone born and raised as a Christian, Muslim, or Hindu, etc. Perhaps Hick means that the religious pluralist is not raised as one, but rather comes to his position via some convincing arguments later on in life. One could say the same thing about religious conversion or an areligious conversion. There are many examples of such conversions, including agnostic to religious, from religious exclusivist to religious pluralist, from religious exclusivist to atheist, from atheist to religious pluralist, etc.[13] So though Hick claims that the cases between a) a religious exclusivist who was raised at birth and from the surrounding culture as a religious exclusivist, and b) a religious pluralist are "so different the analogy fails," he has given no such argument for *why* they are different.[14] Given that there are numerous examples of someone converting from several religious or areligious positions to another, it seems that there is some prima facie evidence that Hick is mistaken and that Plantinga's analogy does not fail. Hick's objections do not amount to a defeater for the Christian exclusivist or any other form of religious exclusivism.

RETROSPECTION

I have been arguing throughout this work that the diversity of religious views present in the world today do not constitute a defeater for Plantinga's Reformed Epistemological defense of Christian exclusivism. Consider again the first premise of my main argument:

---

12. The verification principle claimed that for a non-analytic (i.e., true by definition, etc.) sentence to be meaningful, the sentence must be in principle able to be verified as true or false. Of course the verification principle itself cannot meet that standard of verification. Clifford's principle is as follows: it is wrong always, everywhere, and for anyone, to believe anything upon insufficient evidence. Like the verification principle, Clifford's principle cannot meet its own standard. What sort of evidence or argument would support such a statement? There is none.

13. Mortimer Adler is one example of a philosopher who went from agnosticism to Christian exclusivism.

14. Hick, "Epistemological Challenge of Religious Pluralism," 281.

1. If Plantinga's proper function account is a reasonable account of warrant, then rival religious views to CE do not serve as a defeater to Christian belief having warrant.

I argued in chapter 2 that Plantinga's conclusion that PC is reasonable. Even with the challenge of Bonjour's arguments against moderate foundationalism, I've also argued in chapter 2 that the proper function account of warrant is reasonable given Plantinga's goal of defending CE.

Consider the second premise of my main argument:

2. If rival religious views to CE do not serve as a defeater to Christian belief having warrant, then Plantinga's Reformed Epistemological defense of CE is reasonable.

In chapter 3 I argued that the Problem of Religious Diversity is epistemically deficient since it relies on the equal weight theory. Hence, PRD does not serve as a defeater to Christian belief having warrant. In chapters 4 and 5 I argued that both DeRose's anti-Plantinga argument (PQ) and Willard's internalist criterion argument (WP) are lacking and thus do not serve as defeaters to Christian belief having warrant. I've also argued that neither Baker's nor Hick's account derail Plantinga's Reformed Epistemological defense of Christian Belief. Thus the conclusion of my main argument is:

3. If Plantinga's proper function account is a reasonable account of warrant, then Plantinga's Reformed Epistemological defense of CE is reasonable.

Throughout this work I have argued that someone can hold to a belief even when 1) someone cannot produce a convincing argument that shows her belief is more likely than its rivals, and 2) even when there exist epistemic peers who hold to a conflicting belief. I have also argued that none of the objections aimed at Plantinga's Reformed Epistemological defense of Christian belief succeed in providing a defeater for Christian belief. Though I have not argued that Christian belief is true, I have argued that rival religious views to CE do not serve as a defeater to Christian belief having warrant if Plantinga's proper function account is a reasonable account of warrant. The Christian exclusivist, until someone offers a non-controversial argument that Christian belief is false, can continue to hold to her belief that PC—if Christian belief is true, then it likely is warranted. She can hold to her belief that CE even with the existence of mutually exclusive beliefs and even when she has no argument that would convince someone who disagrees with her. Her cognitive faculties are functioning properly even while she holds to her Christian exclusivism.

Bibliography

Alston, William. *Perceiving God: The Epistemology of Religious Experience.* Ithaca, NY: Cornell University Press, 1991.

Anderson, C. Anthony. "Some Emendations of Gödel's Ontological Proof." *Faith and Philosophy* 7 (1990) 291–303.

Armstrong, D. M. *Belief, Truth, and Knowledge.* London: Cambridge University Press, 1973.

Ayer, A. J. *Language, Truth and Logic.* New York: Dover, 1952.

Baker, Deane-Peter. "Plantinga's Reformed Epistemology: What's the Question?" *International Journal for Philosophy of Religion* 57 (2005) 77–103.

Basinger, David. "Pluralism, and Justified Religious Belief." *Faith and Philosophy* 8 (1991) 67–80.

Beilby, James. *Epistemology as Theology.* London: Ashgate, 2005.

Bonjour, Laurence. *The Structure of Empirical Knowledge.* Cambridge: Harvard University Press, 1985.

Burge, Tyler. "Perceptual Entitlement." *Philosophy and Phenomenological Research* 67 (2003) 503–48.

Carnap, Rudolf. "Empiricism, Semantics, and Ontology." *Revue Internationale de Philosophie* 4 (1950) 20–40.

D'Costa, Gavin. "The Impossibility of a Pluralist View of Religions." *Religious Studies* 32 (1996) 223–32.

DeRose, Keith. "Voodoo Epistemology." Online: http://www.calvin.edu/academic/philosophy/virtual_library/articles/derose_keith/voodoo_epistemology.pdf.

Fales, Evan. "Critical Notice of *Warranted Christian Belief* by Alvin Plantinga." *Nous* 37 (2003) 353–70.

Fitting, Melvin. *Types, Tableaus, and Gödel's God.* Dordrecht: Kluwer Academic 2002.

Gödel, Kurt. "Ontological Proof." In *Collected Works: Unpublished Essays & Lectures*, vol. 3, 403–4. Oxford: Oxford University Press, 1995.

Hazen, A. P. "On Gödel's Ontological Proof." *Australasian Journal of Philosophy* 76 (1998) 361–77.

Hick John. "The Epistemological Challenge of Religious Pluralism." *Faith and Philosophy* 14 (1997) 277–85.

Kelly, Thomas. "The Epistemic Significance of Disagreement." In *Oxford Studies in Epistemology*, edited by John Hawthorne et al. Oxford: Oxford University Press, 2005.

Lewis, David. "Scorekeeping in a Language Game." *Journal of Philosophical Logic* (1979) 339–59.

Mackie, John. *Ethics: Inventing Right and Wrong.* Oxford: Penguin, 1977.

Martin, Michael. *Atheism: A Philosophical Justification.* Philadelphia: Temple University Press, 1990.

Nozick, Robert. "Newcomb's Problem and Two principles of Choice." In *Essays in Honor of Carl G. Hempel*, edited by Nicholas Rescher et al., 114–46. Dordrecht: Reidl, 1969.

Plantinga, Alvin. "A Defense of Religious Exclusivism." In *The Rationality of Belief and the Plurality of Faith*, edited by Thomas Senor, 191–215. Ithaca, NY: Cornell University Press, 1995.

———. "Ad Hick." *Faith and Philosophy* 14 (1997) 295–98.

———. *God and Other Minds*. Ithaca, NY: Cornell University Press, 1967.

———. "Reason and Belief in God." In *Faith and Philosophy*, edited by Alvin Plantinga et al. South Bend: University of Notre Dame Press, 1986.

———. *Warrant and Proper Function*. Oxford: Oxford University Press, 1993.

———. *Warrant: The Current Debate*. Oxford: Oxford University Press, 1993.

———. *Warranted Christian Belief*. Oxford: Oxford University Press, 2000.

Pollock, John. *Contemporary Theories of Knowledge*. Towato: Rowman & Littlefield, 1986.

Russell, Bertrand. *Human Knowledge: Its Scope and Limits*. London: Allen & Unwin, 1948.

Sobel, Jordan Howard. "Gödel's Ontological Proof." In *On Being and Saying. Essays for Richard Cartwright*, edited by Judith Jarvis Thomson, 241–61. Cambridge: MIT Press, 1987.

Smith, Wilfred Cantwell. *Religious Diversity*. New York: Harper & Row, 1976.

Stanford Encyclopedia of Philosophy. "Religious Diversity (Pluralism)." Online: http://plato.stanford.edu/entries/religious-pluralism.

Swinburne, Richard. *The Existence of God*. Oxford: Oxford University Press, 1991.

———. "Plantinga on Warrant." *Religious Studies* 37 (2001) 203–14.

Weatherson, Brian. "Disagreeing about Disagreement." Online: http://brian.weatherson.org/DaD.pdf.

Wikipedia. "Newcomb's Paradox." Online: http://en.wikipedia.org/wiki/Newcomb's_paradox.

Willard, Julian. "Plantinga's Epistemology of Religious Belief and the Problem of Religious Diversity." *Heythrop Journal* XLIV (2003) 275–93.